I WILL BUILD MY CHURCH

Ten Case Studies

of

Church Growth in Taiwan

I WILL BUILD MY CHURCH

TEN CASE STUDIES OF CHURCH GROWTH IN TAIWAN

by

Ten members of
the
Taiwan Church
Growth Society

Allen J. Swanson
Editor

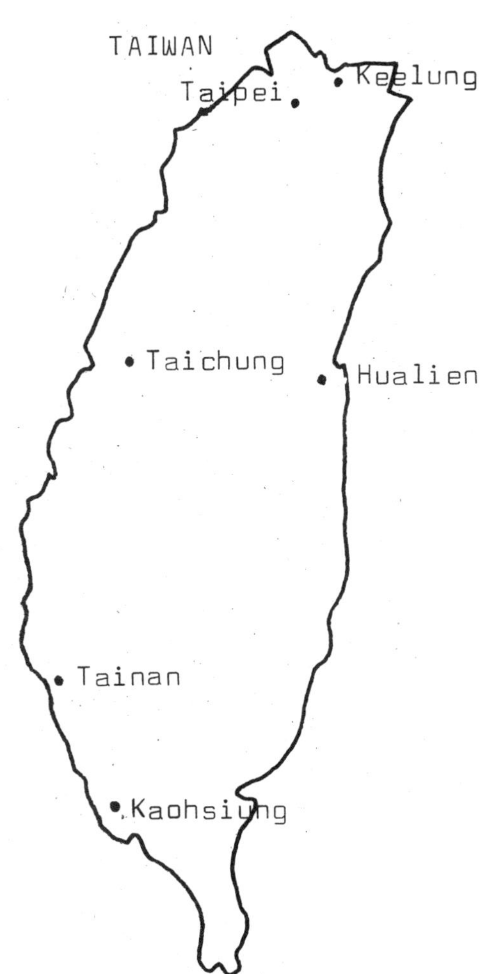

William Carey Library

DEDICATED

to

All our fellow-workers with God,

- past, present and future -

sent

to plant and water

the

Church on Taiwan

with the prayer that God will give the growth.

International Standard Book Number: 0-87808-159-3
Library of Congress Catalog Number: 77-77379

Published by the Taiwan Church Growth Society
P. O. Box 165
Taichung, Taiwan, ROC #400

Printed in Taiwan by MeiYa Publications, Inc.

Available in Taiwan and Asia from:
Spiritual Fountain Book Room
P. O. Box 123
Taichung, Taiwan ROC #400

Available in the U.S. from
William Carey Library
1705 No. Sierra Bonita Ave.
Pasadena, California 91104

TABLE OF CONTENTS

FOREWORD

The book which the Ten Taiwan Church Growth Men have authored
marks a new era in church growth. Each tells the story of a congregation which <u>grew</u>. Each is a trained missiologist. He writes with
insight and accuracy.

Consequently the book presents accounts of what God has in fact
blessed to the growth of His churches in contemporary Taiwan. We
read not of theory which ought to work, but what has in fact worked.
We see the matrix in which each congregation grew. We observe the
part played by the pastor, the laymen, the missionary, local funds,
funds from sister churches, preaching, teaching, healing, and praying. With these ten models before us the task of discipling <u>ta
ethne</u> in Taiwan seems reasonable and possible, interesting and fruitful. We not only hear Christ's command, but also see how His servants have carried it out.

The book will be produced in Chinese. The next task in church
growth thinking is to get multitudes of church growth books in the
major languages of earth, so the heightened faith and obedience to
the church growth movement are shared by and enriched by the thousands of leaders in hundreds of different segments of the Church.

The book will also come out in English. The encouraging stories
of these Chinese churches will be read far and wide around the world.
The Chinese contribution will make us all richer. Furthermore, this
new departure in church growth thinking will be widely copied. We
can look for similar books from many lands with accounts of how new
congregations were in fact brought to birth, nurtured, grew strong,
and went on to give birth to grandsons and granddaughters.

I commend this book. Buy it. Read it. Go and do likewise.

February 2nd, 1977   Donald McGavran
                                            School of Missions
                                            Fuller Seminary, Pasadena, Ca.

Acknowledgements

It is always easier to write a book alone, but it is never as rewarding! This is a case study book of how ten different churches in Taiwan grow. It is the result of the combined efforts of many people - writers and pastors, missionaries and lay people, Westerners and Chinese. It is a true "labor of love." Few of the pastors in this book know much about "church growth theory," but that is irrelevant. What is important is that their churches grow and we want more people to know why they grow. Thus the writers and these church leaders alike have but one prayer - that the Church in Taiwan might realize greater growth and that this book might, in some small way, contribute to this growth.

This book also speaks to others beyond Taiwan. People from other countries who read this book can gain helpful insights into some of the methods God honors in producing church growth. We also hope that other "Church-growth" orientated missionaries will follow suit and produce case studies of how churches grow in their countries.

To bring this book to the press was no small task. Deadlines were usually met under real pressure. As with all special projects, the bulk of the work was done amidst already full schedules. To complicate matters, this book was simultaneously translated into Chinese. Yet everyone cheerfully cooperated.

It would be impossible to give due credit to everyone who helped in this project. The writers receive credit through their by-line at the end of each chapter. The translators are also given credit in the appropriate places. Others also deserve special credit and thanks for their invaluable contributions. The English editors were Miss Vivian Adams and Mrs. Leveta Knox Bentley. Just days before Miss Adams was to return her three manuscripts, her home along with the manuscripts was destroyed by fire. In spite of her own personal loss, she was still willing to re-do the work. Mrs. Bentley, who edited the balance and did the proof-reading, gave long hours of service far beyond the call of "editorial duty." The typists who skillfully put all the parts together were Mrs. Susan Campbell and Mrs. Lily Chen. Mr. Melvin Penner volunteered his services to handle the financial matters - a good deal of the

initial revenue for this book came from trusting writers and sup-
porters who "invested" in this untried project. We believe their
faith will not be in vain. To all of the above, without which
this project would never have been done, our deepest thanks and
appreciation for their loyalty and labor.

The guiding hand for this book rested with a committee of five.
I am deeply indebted to the other four who worked with me. These
co-laborers in the faith are: Dr. Alan Gates, Dr. William Yang,
Tung-chuan, Rev. William Luo, Jung-kuang and Rev. Hans Vandenberg.
They, with me, rejoice in His name at the completion of this task.

Most of all we want to thank the churches and the pastors
whose stories are found within. We are excited that their stories
are being told, and that we had a small part in the telling of
them. They were most gracious and helpful. Many lay people also
offered their time and insights. We are fully aware that their
willingness to open their hearts and churches to public scrutiny
is to invite a host of problems from those who might not agree with
us. But still they welcomed us, in spite of their very busy schedules. Thank you pastors, lay leaders and fellow Christians from
these ten growing churches. Thank you for what you have taught us
writers. Thank you for your love and inspiration. May our Lord
Jesus Christ continue to honor your ministries and increase your
harvests. And may He raise up many more men in Taiwan and beyond
who will follow in your vision and build up the Body of Christ —
unto His honor and glory!

Allen J. Swanson
Coordinating Director
Taiwan Church Growth Society
    Publications Committee
Taipei, Taiwan #111

April 5, 1977

CHURCHES DO GROW IN TAIWAN!
Allen J. Swanson

How do churches grow in Taiwan today? Why do some churches
grow while others do not, often in the same community? As any
student of church growth knows, growth is a complex story involving many factors. Some are man-made; some are determined by the
spirit and mind of God.

Why for example, does one worker labor long in prayer and yet
see little result? Another, while not neglecting prayer, nevertheless sees more fruit, with less prayer. It would seem that prayer
alone does not determine the amount of the harvest.

Again, a highly-trained pastor labors long and hard, with little result. Another man, with no Bible school or seminary training,
produces a healthy, growing church. Apparently seminary training
in itself does not determine the size of the harvest.

Again, several evangelical churches move into a community and,
after a long, dry period with no results, close their doors and
leave. Another church moves in and experiences exciting growth in
less than five years. Why? Apparently the tools and methods we
use have at least as much bearing on our harvest as does the nature
or quality of the soil.

Another church firmly believes in working with the "leaders of
tomorrow"--the youth of today. But their church growth is unstable.
Another church neglects "tomorrow's leaders" and concentrates on
today's leaders--the adults. That church grows, and brings in
"tomorrow's leaders" as well.

We could go on. The questions and illustrations are many. It
is sufficient to note how complex church growth really is. Intensive study can shatter many of our preconceived notions of how

churches grow--or ought to grow!

In the summer of 1976 the Taiwan Church Growth Society Executive Committee began to ask what we could do to make a more effective contribution to the growth of the church in Taiwan. This book is our answer. We asked how could we make a contribution to the Chinese churches and to the missionaries working with these churches. There are many faithful servants of God in Taiwan, from both East and West. They have worked long and hard. Many have gone forth weeping, bearing seed for sowing. But not all have come home with shouts of joy, bringing their sheaves with them (Ps. 126:6). Some have quit. Others have returned to their homeland. Some feel growth is almost impossible at the present. Others wait in faith for a "break-through" or spiritual revival to sweep Taiwan.

All of us in Taiwan are aware of at least some growing churches. Few however, know why they are growing. To be sure, the story of church growth in Taiwan is not as dramatic as some of the illustrations that come from Korea, Indonesia or the Philippines. But there are exciting churches here and there are dramatic break-throughs. The presence of these growing churches presents a challenge. How can we unlock some of their growth secrets and share them with the larger Christian community? More research was needed to understand their reasons for growth. Theories of what "ought to work" we had in abundance. This time our Society wanted to know what does work!

Why are the dynamics of growing churches so little understood? For the missionary, the answer is simple. He simply is not "where the action is." The exciting, healthy church often employs no missionary. It doesn't need one! And so the missionary trods along on the edges, often unaware of the growth dynamics around him. National pastors have the same problem. Burdened with heavy schedules and much "good work," they have little time to visit growing churches, much less analyze their reasons for growth.

With over a dozen graduates of the Fuller Theological Seminary, Institute of Church Growth, residing in Taiwan, we realized we had a potential team of researchers. We only needed to get organized. Although few missionaries are pastoring churches in Taiwan, many are familiar with the church and have church planting experience. Moreover, the missionary, because of his foreign background, can

bring a certain objective research ability to his task. He can
move in more readily than is often possible for our local colleagues.
He can dare to ask the "whys and wherefores" that go with digging
out the facts. He is less likely to be rebuffed by local church
leaders not too interested in sharing their insights with curious
outsiders.

The task of selecting a typical cross section of churches in
Taiwan was not easy. This book makes no pretence to being a final,
authoritative word on how all churches grow in Taiwan. Some exciting
stories are not recorded within these pages. We faced many questions. For example, should we include a cross section that represents all the important elements in Taiwan's Church and cultural
background? Should we include both rural and urban case studies?
How should we decide between Taiwanese and Mandarin-speaking churches?
What about the Hakka churches and the many tribal churches scattered
throughout the mountains of Taiwan? And what about the strange work
of the Holy Spirit in some of these churches that has brought sudden new life to some of the formerly weak mountain churches? Should
this story also be told in so few case studies? Gradually we set
up the following criteria:

1. Gather references of growing churches from as many sources
as possible. Suggestions came from personal acquaintances, church
and mission leaders, former study projects made by students of
church growth in various seminaries and from seminary teachers in
contact with numerous churches. Each reference included a one-
paragraph sketch outlining the major reasons for considering this
a growing church. Our original list had over thirty churches.

It is important to note that certain well-known, large churches
are not included in this study. We deliberately sought to avoid
"big name" churches. We did not want the average pastor to measure
himself against "the best" of Taiwan's leaders, men who possessed
unusual qualifications that gave their churches almost guaranteed
growth. Rather, we sought to find "average" churches shepherded
by "average men"--men we could identify with. There are no "super-
churches" in this book, no dramatic stories of "men of faith" who
tower over others. These are stories about humble, common men whom
God has used to raise up inspiring churches. We can identify with
them, no matter what our race or culture, for what they have

discovered applies to all men everywhere. Thus this book is not
just a book about Chinese churches written for Chinese. It is a
book about God's church, written for all men everywhere.

2. Reduce the list to ten churches. An editorial committee
of three missionaries and two national pastors acted as a steering
committee for the entire project. We alone accept responsibility
for the final selections made. Many will object to our choice of
churches. We are most aware of the fact that many churches can
claim better records than some of the churches listed in this book.
But in a land of 2,000 churches, it is not possible to be entirely
fair to everyone. We sought to base our final decisions on the
following criteria:

a. Mountain churches would have to be eliminated as there
were too many special factors involved in their growth.

b. Rural churches were eliminated as there were proportion-
ately far fewer strong churches from which to choose.

c. A balance was to be sought between Mandarin-speaking and
Taiwanese-speaking churches. Approximately forty-five percent of
all churches use Taiwanese, about thirty-five percent use Mandarin
and the balance use either the Hakka dialect or one of the mountain
languages. Our final selection included six Taiwanese churches,
three Mandarin churches and one Hakka church. In our original list
of references, we were surprised to note the large number of Taiwanese-speaking churches in our list. Although we have tradition-
ally claimed up to ten percent of the Mandarin community as Christian, as against only one and a half percent of the Taiwanese community, it would seem that today's strongest churches are often
found among the Taiwanese-speaking community. The 112 year history
of the Presbyterian church in Taiwan contributes to this stability.
The Mandarin Church, with only twenty-five to thirty years of history in Taiwan, does not yet reflect the maturity or depth of the
older Taiwanese Church.

d. A balance was sought between denominational and non-
denomination churches from the independent group that make up almost one-third of the Protestant community. 'The Assembly Hall and
True Jesus churches, in spite of their growth, were not included
because of their lack of contact with the larger Christian community. The Presbyterians constitute about fifty percent of all the

other churches in Taiwan. Thus, our final selection includes four
Presbyterian churches, four churches of other denominations, and
two local churches with no denominational affiliation.

3. After reducing our list to ten through much cross-checking,
we assigned churches to each of the writers. Writers were expected
to visit the church as many times as was necessary to secure adequate information. Worship and other services were attended. The
pastor was closely interviewed and the final manuscript was subject
to his approval. Lay leaders, youth and others were also interviewed. Records were consulted where available. A critical evaluation was made by the observer. Some used questionnaire sheets and
other interviewing techniques.

4. After the original draft was completed, the paper was cir-
culated to the other members of the Society who added their critical observations. The paper was then rewritten and sent to an editor for final polishing. Along the way a copy was sent to various
translators for the Chinese edition of this book and that manuscript
followed the same course of action as did the English edition. The
articles written by local Chinese writers were first done in their
native language and then translated for the purposes of this English
edition.

A word of caution now needs to be noted. The writers are all
aware of the fact that these churches are not "models" for all times.
We are aware of their weaknesses for no church is perfect. A summary of these observable weaknesses is listed in the closing chapter. We are aware that there are many who will know these churches
better than the writer and will obviously find fault with our analysis. We offer these case studies for what they are worth and believe that their merits justify their inclusion in this study, whatever the inner faults of the church may be. We therefore urge all
readers to accept these studies in the spirit of good-will in which
they are offered. We are not blind to their weaknesses. Rather,
we praise God for the fact that He does indeed use weak and foolish
men to accomplish His glorious purposes!

At least one study is included not because it is currently a
growing church but because it was a growing church but is no more.
Like many fellow churches in very similar situations, we believe
it has a lesson to offer others. Criticism of another's work is

very easy. What is not so easy is to humbly learn from one another.
It is hoped that these case studies will be received in this spirit
of humility, thankful for what God is doing - through churches just
like yours!

To the many good pastors whose churches merit inclusion in
this book but did not get included, we offer only our apologies.
It would be wonderful to give full credit to all of God's choice
men in Taiwan, but this is impossible. We have merely tried to
choose churches which are representative. We believe that most
church growth in Taiwan today can be traceable to factors spelled
out in some of the following ten studies. We have tried, for example, to deal with such common problems as the following:

"We know some urban churches can grow but that is only because
they gather up the sheep that have migrated from other parts of Taiwan, often the rural areas." In this book we show churches that
do not just rely on "transfer growth" but rather grow because people
are turning to Christ in the urban setting and "conversion growth"
forms the basis of their church.

"We know it is good to 'mobilize the laity' but what if they
do not want to be mobilized? The burden of the church today rests
on the shoulders of over-worked pastors." The following case studies offer ample evidence that the laity of Taiwan's churches <u>can</u>
be mobilized, given proper inspiration, training and guidance. It
is a lesson worthy of close attention!

"Self-support is very difficult for many churches today. The
laity just don't give as they ought. To whom can we turn when the
Mission no longer wants to help us out?" The following case studies
offer ample evidence of churches that are self-supporting, often
from their earliest childhood. Their example can well be studied
by many churches struggling with the problem of self-support.

"The Church in Taiwan today is weak, small, divided and incapa-
ble of much growth." Read the following studies and decide for yourself if this is really the case.

But, in spite of all the emphasis on "growth dynamics," two
factors stand out clearly and need underscoring. First, as we read
the story told by each church, we are struck with the awareness of
the power and presence of God in their midst! Jesus Christ is indeed Lord of their churches - and their lives! They all have a

certain "urgency" about them, they "must get the message out!" They
know that they have been appointed stewards of this grace - to be
shared with others. That is one reason why they grow. All the
methods in the world are useless without that inner desire to share
the Good News!

Second, we note the importance of leadership! It is a key if
not the key! Churches grow or die on the basis of the leadership
at the top! Are you leaders listening? This is where the logjam
often lies! Outdated methods, adherence to fruitless programs, a
sterile spiritual life, indifference, inertia and an over-occupation
with marginal tasks are all part of the devil's plot to sidetrack
us from the issue of church growth. And often the leaders fall vic-
tim to this trap! I have taught enough church growth courses to
enthusiastic Christian young people to realize how frustrated they
become over the inability of the leadership to accept new ideas and
methods. They are not just students. Many have secular occupations.
They study through extension education classes. They long to see
more growth. This frustration of a new, enlightened younger generation of Christian youth is exciting--if it can be channeled into
healthy church growth programs.

But when God wants to build His church, He always begins with a
man--a man with a vision and a burden, a man with a deep desire to
honor the Lord, a passion to lead others to Him and to follow the
principles of church growth found in the New Testament. He is not
a slave to tradition or denominational formulas. He seeks to communicate Truth and will not tolerate the restricting of this call
through endless programs that create more branches than fruit. And
he knows how to inspire others, for he knows that God never calls
a man to work alone. All the gifts needed are found in the Body,
and as their leader he must utilize all of these gifts for the
upbuilding of God's church.

Church growth is exciting. Being with growing churches and
leaders of growing churches is an honor. If this book can in some
way inspire others to catch the vision of what God can do through
them, if they too can discover how their church can grow, then this
book will not have been written in vain. And so we offer this up
as token of our faith in God, in His Church, and in the men whom
He calls.

Chapter 1

PEACE-AND-JOY

PRESBYTERIAN

CHURCH:

KEELUNG'S CHURCH

WITH OPEN DOORS!

Pastor Cho Hui-lung

Traversing Keelung's <u>Hsi Ting</u> Road the visitor comes upon an
old, pink-walled church with green-painted doors and windows. The
main building, built in 1950, is almost out-dated as cracks in its
main walls are discernable. A steeple also pink in color topped
by the Christian cross accents the buildings. The cross marks the
premises as a Christian center. It is precisely this, for its doors
to the main auditorium are open from six in the morning until ten
at night every day of the week.

Here at the An-le Presbyterian Church Christian believers and
seekers after truth can find a place for private prayer or receive
counselling from the pastor, a deacon or an elder. Students may
enter upper rooms in the church complex with reserved tables and
seats for a place of quiet study or, on occasion, a game of ping-
pong. Two hundred children attend the Peace-Joy Christian kindergarten, a school well equipped with a playground and adequate classrooms in a two-storey building to the left of the church complex.
Connecting the church and the kindergarten is a guest hall, a building said to be erected eighty years ago with thick walls and

old-time fixtures.

The main church edifice, student center and guest hall will give way in time to a new modern structure, housing a church auditorium planned to seat a thousand, a larger student center than the present one and even a church morgue to facilitate Christian funerals. The Reverend Cho Hui-lung, the pastor, speaks glowingly of these present plans and adds that the "living Christians will come in by the main entrance stairs and literally 'ascend' to the House of the Lord. Deceased believers will be tendered with care in the morgue and will be escorted through the side doors out to the surrounding hillsides for burial." The vision to build a new church to seat a thousand initially came from a 64-year-old deacon in the An-le Church. This sparked a flame in Pastor Cho's heart, for he immediately concurred.

"PEACE-AND-JOY" CHURCH

One can thus readily detect zeal and reverence for the House of the Lord upon the part of this vibrant pastor and the believers of this unique church. This zeal and reverence is noted in two Scriptures taken from the Psalms that grace the weekly bulletin. They are as follows:

> "I was glad when they said to me, 'Let us go to the House
> of the Lord.'"
> "How lovely is Thy dwelling place, O Lord of hosts!"
> (Psalms 122:1; 84:1).

As to the name of the church - the An-le Presbyterian Church - Pastor Cho explained: "We called it 'An' for <u>Peace</u> and 'Lok' (Le in Mandarin Chinese) for <u>Joy</u>, for both peace and joy are found in Christ and in His Gospel!"

FOUNDING HISTORY

How was the An-le Presbyterian Church founded? Actually, it had its antecedents in early Presbyterian church-planting in Keelung, as early as 1875, by the intrepid Canadian missionary-pioneer: Dr. George L. MacKay.

It began through the contacts of a Taiwanese Christian, Ko Chin, a remarkable convert who had heard Dr. MacKay preach elsewhere. Ko Chin, baptized at the age of 45, rented and furnished a house

for a church in his home-city of Keelung and invited MacKay to come.
When MacKay preached the dedicatory services there, more than 400
were present. Ko Chin later was ordained an elder in the Keelung
Church. This was the first-fruits of what developed into the Kee-
lung Presbyterian Church. During its hundred-year-old history this
church has mothered _nine_ other Presbyterian churches in the city
(MacKay 1895:157-158; Presbyterian Church in Taiwan 1971:11-12;
Hwang, ed. 1972:424).

One of these nine churches became known as the An-le Presbyterian Church. In 1949, although the city of Keelung had at that
time at least eight Presbyterian churches, a group of believers
and some elders of a small preaching mission petitioned leaders of
their denomination to send them a pastor to start a new Presbyterian
church in their area. They directly approached Pastor Cho Hui-lung,
then teaching at the Tamkang Christian School in Tanshui, and confronted him with the question: "Are you going to be a pastor of a
church, or are you going to continue to be a teacher for the rest
of your life?" Pastor Cho took this as the challenge that he needed
and subsequently moved to Keelung to start what became a most fruitful ministry.

PASTOR CHO

Pastor Cho's background is enriched with four generations of
Christian ancestry. His father, an outstanding man with fifty years
in the ministry, had in his early years been an associate of Dr.
George MacKay. A photograph of the father is prominently displayed
in the guest hall of the An-le Church. This father's maternal grandmother was the earliest of the Cho clan to hear the Gospel message,
who evidently received it from the "Black-bearded Barbar' ' himself
(as Dr. MacKay was sometimes called).

Pastor Cho studied under Dr. George William MacKay, principal
of the Presbyterian school in Tanshui and the son of the f rst MacKay.
An older brother of Pastor Cho preceded him in the ministr . Pastor
Cho furthered his education at the Taiwan Presbyterian Seminary in
Greater Taipei and at the Shen Ta-hsueh Shen Hsueh Yuan in Kobe,
Japan. Seminary training enhanced his gifts for his forthcoming ministry.

Prior to the three years of teaching at Tanshui, Pastor Cho
had pastored in Chin-k'uang, a gold-mining town (as the name suggests)

and at Chiu-fen, another town in northern Taiwan. These were years
of Japanese control in Taiwan, then popularly known as Formosa to
the outside world. During the years of World War II Pastor Cho was
closely watched by the Japanese authorities who thought him to be
a spy of the Westerners. In 1945 police arrested him and imprisoned
him for a period of two months. In refusing to bow to the Shinto
shrine he had made himself all the more conspicuous. With poor food
and rough treatment his health began to give out. The authorities
condemned him to die. In his desperation he earnestly prayed and
vowed that were the Lord to deliver him, he would "give his life
to the Lord and to His service until the day of his decease."

Almost at the breaking point in his suffering, deliverance finally came. In August, 1945 atomic bombs fell upon Japanese cities
and the nation surrendered to the Allies. Following the cessation
of hostilities leaders of the victorious nations met at Potsdam for
an important international conference. A significant outcome of
this conference for Taiwan and for Pastor Cho was that Japan released
her hold upon the island and Taiwan reverted back to Chinese rule.
This political turnover spelled freedom for Pastor Cho just in the
nick of time. Upon the return of Dr. George MacKay to Taiwan after
the war, Pastor Cho was invited to teach at Tanshui.

Thus it was a concerned nucleus of Presbyterian believers and
elders and Pastor Cho together who founded the An-le Presbyterian
Church. This church-planting was backed by the Presbyterian Synod.
Dr. MacKay, though losing a teacher, gave Pastor Cho his blessing.
The Keelung Presbyterian Church, the oldest in the city, as we have
noted, directed fifteen families to the new church to give it self-
support right from the time of its official inception.

There was one misgiving factor in Pastor Cho's going to Keelung
to pastor this new church. This was the city's rainy, humid climate,
more severe even than that of Tanshui. Keelung, surrounded by hills,
is located in the windward side of a mountain range where precipi-
tation causes a very rainy climate - the rainiest in the country.
However, undaunted by the climate, Pastor Cho and his family moved
to Keelung. Upon exercising faith for his own healing and in praying for sick people in Keelung, his own TB-strickened body received
a Divine touch. His life became a living miracle! He has kept
alive the wonder of this past experience to inspire his own faith

as well as that of his people.

THE FIRST SERVICE

"Noah Believed and His Whole Family Entered the Ark," Such
was the title of the first message preached by Pastor Cho on the
morning of October 9, 1949 with 24 present. Records of that service still extant show that the offering received amounted to $41
wan! (about NT$200 now). This was a time when the paper currency
had rapidly fallen in value. Pastor Cho's sermon topic was significant, for in subsequent years, he was to witness many Taiwanese
families who, like Noah and his family, would enter the Ark of
safety and place their trust in the Savior, Christ Jesus.

FAMILY CONVERSIONS AND IDOL DESTRUCTION

During the first year of his ministry at the newly-founded
church Pastor Cho led six new families to Christ. After their conversions they promptly destroyed their idols. Later, nineteen additional families claimed Christ as Lord and Savior and no longer
worshipped their household gods. During 1950, in each of two baptismal services, nineteen were baptized, adding 38 more persons to
the church.

Over a span of 26 years Pastor Cho witnessed a total of 278
families turn to the Lord and forsake their idols. A notebook of
his handwritten notes entitled "Historical Notes of Idol Destruc-
tion"* carefully numbers and dates these momentous occurrences. In
addition to this rare record, over 1,000 have been baptized in 155
baptismal services!

PRAYER AND MIRACLES

During the first ten years of the history of the church, when
the believers encountered much opposition, the Lord confirmed His
word with miracles. Pastor Cho firmly believes that preachers are
to be sent forth to preach the Gospel and to heal the sick. His
Scriptural stance is based on the words of Luke 9:1-2:

> "He gave them (the twelve disciples) power and authority
> over all demons and to cure diseases, and He sent them
> out to preach the kingdom of God and to heal."

---

*"Ch'u Ou-hsiang Li-shih Ts'e" (Mandarin Chinese)

With this biblical backing Pastor Cho prays for the sick with the
laying on of hands. Believers have commented on the "power of
Jesus Christ coming upon them," when their pastor prays for them
and have experienced spiritual, mental and physical relief.

Many Taiwanese families are troubled by chronic illnesses and
fear of evil spirits that may molest them. Some dread the possibility of natural calamities and accidents. In this environment
Christ's power to save, to heal and to protect is the "Balm of Gil-
ead" to distraught people.

During the early years of the history of An-le Presbyterian
Church an unusual case of deliverance occurred. A family mourned
the sickness and eventually, the death of a much-treasured baby son.
Pastor Cho was called to the home where he heard death lamentations.
With fearless faith he laid his hands upon the still, pale form of
the child and prayed for recovery. The Lord restored life and health
to the boy. Predictably, this miracle brought the whole family into
the fellowship of the church.

AN EDUCATIONAL CENTER

Pastor Cho, in his first few years at An-le, had vision for
an educational center in his church. He founded a kindergarten and
in the beginning even taught the youngsters himself. Bible stories,
made interesting and relevant, caught the attention of parents of
the children. Later, his wife shouldered responsibilities in the
growing kindergarten.

Pastor Cho reached out to the student population of the neighborhood. For a while he taught English as a means to win the young
people. A youth study center was opened and became a vital part of
the outreach of this church. Across the years Pastor Cho personally
instructed Bible classes to indoctrinate students and church workers.
Taiwanese Romanization was taught to the illiterate to enable them
to read the Scriptures and the Presbyterian hymnal, Seng-si, "Holy
Songs." All these emphases in Christian education have paid divi-
dends to the church both numerically, in the growth of the church,
and financially, in offsetting overhead expenses.

A GRAPH OF CHURCH GROWTH

The following chart on page   constructs available data into
a line graph of total church growth across 27 years of the An-le
Church's history. We have noted that 24 people were present in
the first service marking the official beginning of the An-le Church.
The Keelung Presbyterian Church gave 15 families to the infant
church. Reckoning a national average in Taiwan of at least five
members to a family, the total membership including the original
24 amounted to about 100 by the end of 1950. Two baptismal services that we know of added 38 additional members to the church.
In the following two years the addition of six families and then
nineteen families added at least 125 people. By the end of 1952
there were approximately 225 believers in the fellowship of the
church.

From 1952 to 1966 where concrete data is not available, we in-
fer further growth by indirect means. Well over two hundred families coming to Christ during this period, in multi-individual decisions, known as a _people_ _movement_, and subsequently destroying
their idols, swelled the membership into the three hundreds and
four hundreds. Natural increase of children in the now-Christian
families also added to the ranks. One must also consider losses,
encountered in any church of several hundred members, such as mi-
grating out and death. However, in the history of this church,
gains considerably outstripped losses.

One type of loss beneficial to many was the voluntary transfer
of members to form the nuclei of new churches. Over the years the
An-le Church has mothered four branch churches in the general Keelung City area. These have become the following Presbyterian
Churches:

(1)   Chung-cheng Church   -   founded in 1951
(2)   Hsien-tung Chung Shan Church - founded in 1954
(3)   Shih-fen Liao Church   -   founded in 1957
(4)   Ho-p'ing Tao Church   -   founded in 1959

During the last ten years from 1966 to 1976 available data puts
us on factual ground. A peak in the number of believers was reached
by the end of 1971 when the roll stood at 569 (Presbyterian Church
in Taiwan, General Office statistics, 1976; Hwang, ed. 1972:426).

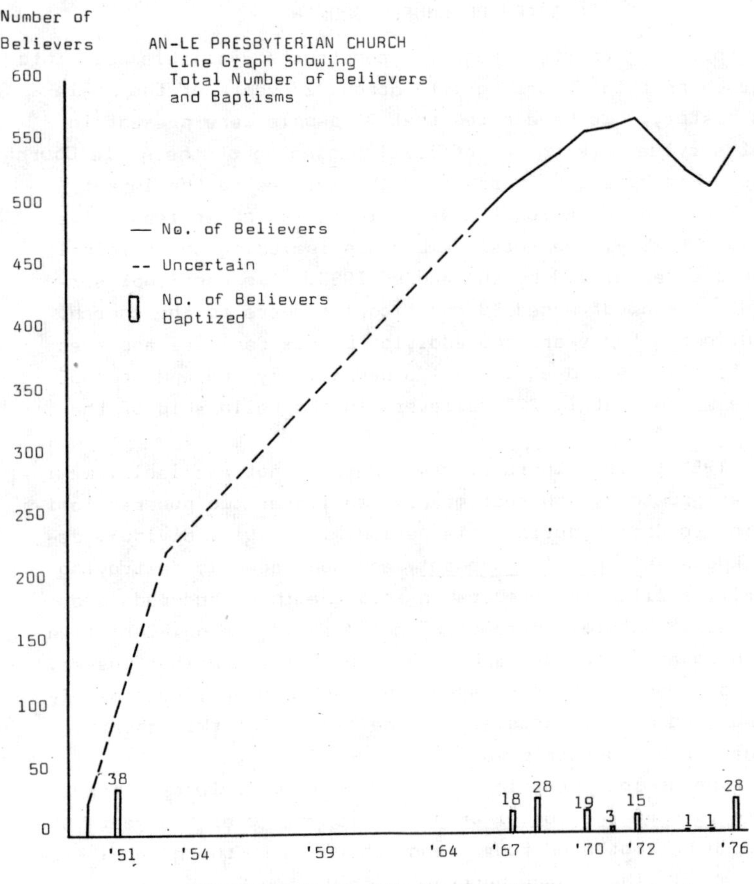

ATTENDANCE AT THE AN-LE CHURCH

The writer attended two Sunday morning worship services in October, 1976. The church auditorium was well filled especially on the left side facing the pulpit. Here, elderly women and young mothers with babies or young children were seated noticeably towards the back of the church. Middle-aged ladies and girls crowded the rest of the seating space. The right side contained mostly men, old and young and middle-aged, boys and a scattering of couples. More than 240 attended each service.

One morning service honored the presence of 31 aged members,

both men and women, 70 years in age and older. Their names were
called by Pastor Cho and presents were given to them as they came
forward. Photos were taken to celebrate the occasion. Members of
the women's society flanked the aged friends on all sides and
aided them in singing a special number.

All the preaching, singing, praying and announcing was in Taiwanese with the exception of a choir number sung in Mandarin Chinese.

Lay participation in the services was obvious. Four individuals: two young deacons and two old elders had part in the beginning and at the end of the service in leading the singing, making
announcements and giving reports. Pastor Cho, forceful in his
preaching, ministered in popular Taiwanese vernacular. He spoke
with great freedom. Special excitement was evident in the plans
for the new church complex and payment of the new electronic organ!

A warm welcome was extended to visitors. All clapped when they
were introduced, and especially when representatives of three generations stood to their feet: a grandfather and elder in An-le, his
son and grandson. A granddaughter of a deceased and honored grandmother was introduced. A memorial house meeting was to be conducted
in honor of the deceased - an effectual substitute in Christian
circles for ancestral worship.

AN ANALYSIS OF THE CONGREGATION

Members of the congregation by-and-large represent a <u>lower
middle class</u> of Taiwanese urban society. They are day laborers,
harbor and warehouse workers, teachers, housewives, public office
workers and students. One informant places the student ratio as
high as one third of those who regularly attend the morning worship
services. No exceptionally wealthy people are here neither are
there any professional personnel such as doctors, dentists or law-
yers. The church is largely comprised of a <u>single homogenous unit</u>
where ordinary urban working-class Taiwanese people feel at home
with each other. Most of these are first-generation Christians.

It is a "family-unit" church whose present community may be
analyzed as follows:

    90 full families at 5 members per family   =   450
    50 half families (where only one parent

                  and one or more children are Christians)
                  at 2.5 members per unit   = 125
          30 to 100 (according to various informants)
                  are single individuals   = 30-100

                          Total <u>community</u> figure   605-675

     The pastor registers his congregation in terms of <u>hu</u>, or family
units, which now numbers approximately 200. This thinking incor-
porates full families, half families and even individuals. Ethnical-
ly, the congregation is composed of 80% Taiwanese, 17% Hakka and
3% Mainlanders who understand Taiwanese.

     According to a demographic study of Keelung published in 1970
by Professor Lung Kwan-hai of the Taiwan National University, the
area in which the An-le Church is located has a population density
ranging from 1,000 to as high as 5,000 persons per square kilometer
(Lung, 1970). Ninety percent of the An-le Church's congregation
lives within one square kilometer of its location. This indicates
that the church has been very effective in reaching a fairly-dense
Taiwanese population within walking and riding distance.

                          CHURCH ORGANIZATION

     All in the church are registered by households as noted above
and are considered as members. However, only those baptized and
of age after confirmation, are entitled to a vote in the business
affairs of the church. The church is well organized under the main
leadership of the pastor. Deacons and elders all have a share in
the responsibilities and administration of the church. The area
surrounding the church is divided into <u>ch'u</u>, meaning districts,
and each <u>ch'u</u> has an elder in charge of both members and contacts.
Every <u>ch'u</u> is subdivided into <u>li</u> and its leader is a deacon, or a
"warm-hearted," that is, zealous believer.

     Five departments are found in the church. The first concerns
itself with evangelism, spiritual life and visitation. The second
is related to education: supervision of the kindergarten, youth
center and Bible studies. The third is the trusteeship of the
property. The fourth has the care of the church supplies, upkeep
of the premises and operation of the church. The fifth involves
special ministries and social concern. The pastor, having a deep
understanding of the religious background of Taiwanese people he

seeks to reach, pays special attention to the conducting of Christian funerals and safeguards his people from the many superstitions pertaining to death. He and his committee help minister to the sick and provide means for the jobless. The pastor delegates work and responsibilities and thus involves his people in the ministries of their church.

DYNAMICS OF GROWTH

When asked what they felt were reasons for growth and success, various informants gave the following answers:

A youth leader said, "The church is of one heart and one mind. All believers, together with the pastor, work with one another for the upbuilding of the church."

Another informant stated that the pastor "willingly delegates the responsibilities of the church to believers who are leaders; therefore all are kept busy and the church grows."

"The main dynamic of growth," acknowledges the pastor himself, "has been the Holy Spirit Who is at work. Were it not for His movings, our church would not be in the place that it is today."

One of the pastor's sons, now in seminary training for the ministry and assisting his father, suggests that the emphasis on "whole families for Christ" is a secret of growth. He adds further, "The women's group of over 40 in number and active in prayer and visitation adds to the strength of the church." Then in the final analysis, he continues, "The pastor himself shepherds the church. He is a man who prays and submits himself to the leading of the Holy Spirit. He meditates near his telephone. When it rings he is alert to respond to needs. If necessary, he is off immediately to visit a home and to offer prayer and counsel."

THE TAIWANESE PASTOR: A KEY TO CHURCH GROWTH

In a research made on conversions among the Taiwanese in 1972, out of a total of 78 first-generation urban converts from a pagan background, 43 named the pastor as the influential agent in their coming to Christ. In addition, a survey made of twelve urban Taiwanese churches planted within the last thirty years revealed the following data: First, twelve informants named the pastor as the

chief agent in church planting. Second, nine out of the twelve
affirmed that it was the vision and burden of a Taiwanese <u>pastor</u>
which made the church planting possible (Bolton 1976:188, 249-250).
The An-le Church's pastor verifies this research. He himself is a
catalyst for church growth.

A TAIWANESE PEOPLE MOVEMENT

Another factor in the dynamic of church growth here is that a
remarkable people movement took place, resulting in 278 families
coming to Christ, destroying their idols and participating in the
spiritual life and numerical development of the church. Bishop
J.W. Pickett who labored many years in India, compares this method
of coming to Christ with the altogether-too-common one-by-one individual type:

> One way of Christianization permits and encourages
> <u>groups</u> of families from <u>within the same people</u> to
> come to salvation <u>without social dislocation</u> in a
> constant and ever-widening stream. Whereas another
> way of Christianization permits and encourages in-
> dividuals of many people having been torn from their
> societies, to come to salvation in an intermittent
> and gradually diminishing trickle (emphases ours,
> Pickett, Warnshuis, Singh and McGavran, 1973:64).

Pastor Cho acknowledges that his people bring in people. He
says, "Believers give birth to believers; the sheep and not the shepherd give birth to sheep." The groups of families coming to Christ
are all Taiwanese-speaking people of the same <u>homogenous</u> unit: a
working class brought into the church without social or cultural
dislocation. This movement substantiates a church growth principle
that people are more apt to come to Christ where the social, linguistic and cultural barriers are not in the way. It has happened
here at the An-le Church.

Most of the 278 families are <u>small</u>, points out Pastor Cho. In
coming to Christ the move to destroy their household gods has naturally come from the people themselves, from the voice of authority
in the household. Sometimes it is that of the husband; other times
it is even that of the wife. Whoever the motivator is, however, the
matter of saying good-by to a household god is not a light affair.
Perhaps the fact that most of these households are small, nuclear
families offers a clue. Larger, extended families, involving at

least two generations, complicates the issue and lessens the possibility of eradicating a clan idol. Too many voices of authority
are involved. Ordinarily, idols are handed down from one generation
to another, and theoretically, they are property of the clan and not
of one single individual.

A FUNCTIONAL SUBSTITUTE FOR IDOLS

Instead of leaving only bare walls, with the elimination of the
colorful idol shelf, idol or idol picture, Pastor Cho offers a functional substitute. He and the church donate a favorite picture of
his, that of Christ praying in the garden of Gethsemane. It serves
to remind the now-Christian family that Christ their Lord and Savior
"intercedes for you and bestows His peace," in the words of their
pastor. To newly-weds Pastor Cho gives a Bible picture text "God
is Love." These pictures and text bear a Christian witness. - Buddhist mendicants going from house to house upon arriving at these
households and seeing these pictorial evidences of Christianity in
a prominent place where god-shelves used to be are inclined to leave
right away!

CASE STUDY OF A FAMILY

How do these Taiwanese families come to Christ? Perhaps a specific case study of a family will help us see the channels through
which the Gospel flows. The chart below accompanies our description.

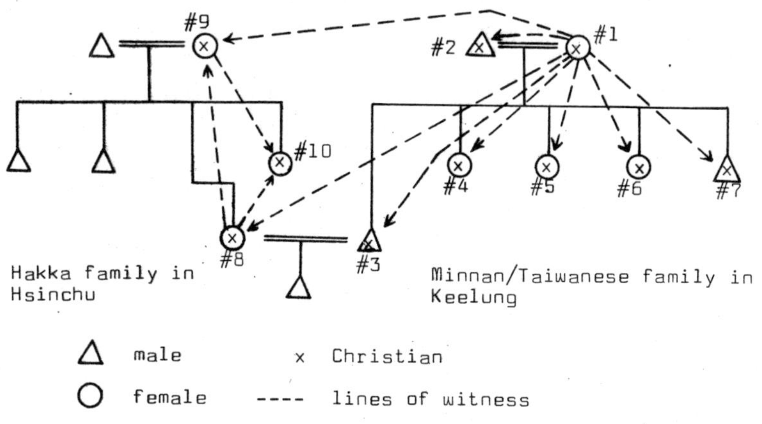

An illiterate wife #1 of a laborer was converted at the An-le
Presbyterian Church under the ministry of Pastor Cho Hui-lung. She
was filled with the Holy Spirit through the influence of a Pente-
costal group and felt urged to witness for the Lord. She won her
husband #2 to Christ, a Taiwanese driver of a three-wheel motorized
cart, one who hauls goods in Keelung city.

Upon his conversion the couple invited Pastor Cho to conduct
house meetings in their home located in Chung San Ch'u, a fair distance away from the church. Other believers and friends and neighbors gathered there from time to time. Their home became a place
for prayer. With this Christian atmosphere in the home the oldest
son #3 was converted. His younger sisters #4, #5, #6 and a younger
brother #7 also were brought to Christ. Thus another Taiwanese
whole family was baptized and added to the An-le Church!

The oldest son #3 married a non-Christian Hakka girl from Hsinchu,
a city about 130 kilometers southwest of Keelung. She was a seam-
stress who did not understand Taiwanese. Undaunted by this linguistic barrier, her mother-in-law #1 showed her love and witnessed to
her. Through this rather unusual treatment the daughter-in-law #8
was won to the Christian faith. She in turn became gracious to her
own immediate family and especially kind to her parents and old folk
in the Hakka clan.

Once her Hakka mother became ill. The Christian daughter #8
and the daughter's mother-in-law #1, on a visit from Keelung, prayed
for her and she was healed. This episode became a turning point in
her life; she accepted Christ as her Savior. The Hakka daughter #8
and her mother #9 became instruments through whom a younger sister
#10 was converted to Christ. Conversion of part of this Hakka family
was not without persecution, however. Once when a Hsinchu Presbyterian pastor came into their home area for evangelistic ministry,
the two older brothers of #8 struck him with several blows!

This case reveals the potential of Gospel witness from a key-
person, influential among her kin, to others through kinship lines.
These lines resemble a spider's web, a web of Chinese kinships, connecting links, over which the message of salvation can be transmitted.
The above account has an unusual touch about it, for not only did
the Gospel flow along kinship lines, but also spread over from the
Taiwanese ethnic group to the Hakka people, and through marriage

from one clan to another.

A RECENT PICTURE OF CHURCH GROWTH

The following facts give us a fairly up-to-date picture of An-le Church's growth. Peak morning worship attendance stood at the 331 mark in 1975. Adult membership was 290. Baptized children added another 222. An additional 32 new converts brought the total number of believers to 544 as of the end of 1975 (Please see graph on page   ).

Though their names are retained in the church membership registry, 50 members have moved away from Keelung, leaving a figure of 462 resident members at the end of 1975. A point suggested here is that names of members leaving a church permanently should be eliminated from the membership roll and should be considered in statistics as those who have transferred out. This suggestion when followed reveals more accurately the actual strength of the church.

A further point to note is the healthy number of inquirers: thirty and above, within the last four years. Inquirers are potential members. Decisions for Christ, indoctrination and baptisms make membership possible.

Church growth statistics giving the number of additions to the church through baptisms and transferring in of Christians, minus the number of losses through death and transferring out of Christians, present a more factual picture of the actual annual net gain. For example, although the An-le Church received 28 new members through baptisms last year, there were 11 losses (6 died and 5 moved away), thus making a net gain of 17 members.

At the end of 1975, the women's group numbered 48, the Sunday school 108, the choir 81 and the youth group 83. Prayer meetings averaged 63 in attendance, house meetings 36 and Sunday evening services 43 during that year (Presbyterian Church in Taiwan, General Office Statistics, 1976).

SUMMARY

The An-le Presbyterian Church offers an excellent example of church planting and growth. Lessons of church growth derived from this study are many. In conclusion, the following ten points are offered for the readers consideration:

1. The pastor sought out the most authoritative member in the
    family and preached the Gospel to him or to her.

2. The pastor, his elders and deacons also sought out families in
    need, in trouble or with illness and counselled with them and
    prayed for them.

3. The pastor has the knack of identifying himself with his
    people and understanding their life-style. He is like the
    prophet Ezekiel who "sat where they (his own people) sat"
    (Ezekiel 3:15). Rapport with people is necessary for church
    growth.

4. Taiwanese society's ritualized highpoints in life such as mar-
    riages, births and deaths are utilized for the witness of the
    Gospel. Life's crises are seized as opportunities to introduce
    Christ as Savior, Comforter and Friend.

5. Pastor Cho found a receptive homogeneous unit in Keelung: a
    working class of urban Taiwanese people. The masses of common,
    ordinary working people are not to be despised, for they are more
    likely to turn to the Christian faith than the aristocratic, self-
    sufficient, upper classes. Let receptivity be a guide in evangelis-
    tic outreach and church-planting.

6. He encouraged whole family units, by multi-individual decisions,
    and with much prior consultation among themselves, to make
    public commitments to Christ. Idol-destroying ceremonies dramatized
    and heightened these decisions.

7. The pastor is willing and has the ability to use laity in organized
    outreach. He delegates the ministries of the church to elders,
    deacons and to dedicated, capable and willing believers.

8. The principle of departmentalization is made use of in the An-le
    Church. The large choir, women's group, youth groups, elders'
    and deacons' corps, junior church members and Sunday school for
    youngsters are examples. Each group has its own leaders and
    measure of organization.

9. Prayer is given priority in the church and in homes of believers.

10. The pastor emphasizes the power and ministry of the Holy Spirit.
    In an environment of polytheistic and animistic folk religion, a
    belief in miracles is relevant. Sick people made well again through

care, concern and healing are grateful and receptive. The Gospel of
Jesus Christ given in the power of the Spirit is the dynamite of God
for salvation to every one who believes (Romans 1:16). Pastor Cho has
found it so in his An-le Church ministry!

SOURCE MATERIAL

AN-LE PRESBYTERIAN CHURCH   Weekly Church Bulletins.
        1976

BOLTON, Robert J.   Treasure Island: Church Growth Among
                                 Taiwan's Urban Minnan Chinese. South
                                 Pasadena, California, William Carey
                                 Library.

CHO, Chung-hui   Interview, Shih-Lin. Son of Pastor
        1976   Cho, Hui-long and student at Taiwan
                                 Theological Seminary.

CHO, Hui-lung   Interviews, Keelung. Pastor of An-le
        1973   Presbyterian Church.
        1976

HWANG, Liu-tien, Ed.   A Century of the Presbyterian Church
        ·1972   in Northern Formosa. Taipei, Taiwan,
                                 Taiwan Presbyterian Church.

LUNG, Kwan-hai   "Population Distribution in the Five
        1970   largest cities in Taiwan," Journal of
                                 Sociology. Taipei, Taiwan, National
                                 Taiwan University.

MacKAY, George Leslie   From Far Formosa. New York, Fleming
        1895   Revell.

PICKET, J.W., WARNSHUIS, A.E.,   Church Growth and Group Conversion.
SINGH, H.G. & McGAVRAN, D.A.   South Pasadena, California, William
        1973   Carey Library.

PRESBYTERIAN CHURCH IN TAIWAN   Taipei, Taiwan, General Office church
        1971   statistics.
        1976

WANG, T'ing   "Chiao-hui Tseng-chang: Tiao-ch'a
        1976   Pao-kao An-le Chiao-hui," Shih-Lin,
                                 China Evangelical Seminary student's
                                 Church Growth class handwritten re-
                                 search paper.

ABOUT THE AUTHOR

Robert J. Bolton was born February 26, 1929 in Kunming, China, the son of the Rev. and Mrs. Leonard G. Bolton, Assemblies of God missionaries for thirty-five years in China, East Pakistan, Burma, Hawaii and Taiwan.

Robert was converted to Christ in early boyhood and called to Christian service in his teens.

He received his B.A. from Central Bible College, Springfield, Missouri, in 1951, and in 1974 received his M.A. degree in Missions at the School of World Mission and Institute of Church Growth of Fuller Theological Seminary, Pasadena, California.

Robert and his wife, Evelyn, have been engaged in evangelizing, church planting and Bible teaching ministries among the Minnan Chinese and aborigines of Taiwan, Republic of China. They are under appointment by the Division of Foreign Missions of the General Council of the Assemblies of God, U.S.A.

Chapter 2

HAKKA

HOME

FELLOWSHIPS

In the Chang home in Chung ko

First on left, Mr. Lai
Third from left, Mrs. Chan
Fifth from left, Mr. Chang

I would like to describe how three Hakka Home Fellowships came
into being near Tungshih in Taichung County in a very unexpected way.

The fellowships are unique in several respects. For one, they
came into existence in a farming area when other country groups were
losing members to the city. They were begun and developed among the
Hakka-speaking Chinese during the time when there was relatively
little outreach to the unsaved in churches of the same ethnic group
in other parts of Taiwan. Another unique aspect is that the ground-
work was laid by a lay person who called the missionary in to help
only after her family was ready to listen to the Gospel. A fourth
variation from most missionary work is that the fellowships are mostly within the web of the lay person's family and friends. A fifth
factor is that the fellowships have continued to be home centered.
This last factor is a very important consideration in reaching the
Hakka - the most conservative of all ethnic groups on Taiwan and the
most fearful of Christianity. Where most churches among all ethnic
groups minister mostly to Christians, two of the Hakka Home

Fellowships continue to have 20 to 50% unsaved in the audience. Perhaps as important as the home in keeping contact with the unsaved, the missionary has wisely guided in making some important functional substitutes. The adaptations have shown the Hakka that Christianity is not a foreign religion but a faith which is applicable to every aspect of Hakka life.

The story of the Hakka Home Fellowships is really the story of Mrs. Chan. She was the oldest sister in the large Yeh family in the Henglung farming area several kilometers north of Tungshih. In 1935 she married a Chinese Medicine salesman. For a few years he had a shop in Tungshih and then moved to Kaohsiung.

Mrs. Chan was troubled by demons from about the time of her marriage and as a result became an ardent worshipper. She gave birth to one daughter and adopted two sons. When the older son was in the army in Chin Men during the concentrated Communist shelling in August 1958, he wrote of the fear that gripped his heart. Mrs. Chan's fear for her son brought on an intensification of demon-filled nightmares.

About that time an elder's wife began visiting Mrs. Chan and inviting her to church. When she heard that slides on the Life of Christ were to be shown, she was finally enticed to go. The demons seized Mrs. Chan in the middle of the showing and she ran out of the meeting. Later the pastor called and told her that she would not get rid of the demons until she believed in God.

Almost two years later Mrs. Chan decided to trust in God. She got up early and began dismantling the worship paraphernalia. A daughter-in-law saw her and thinking it was another demon seizure, called her husband. When several members of the family appeared, she faced them and asked if they could remember any benefit received from worshipping the diagram and idols. No one could think of any benefit so she declared her trust in God and cleared out the worship paraphernalia.

After Mrs. Chan believed, she had a wonderful peace of mind and heart. She was baptized in the Hsin Hsing Presbyterian Church in Kaohsiung and attended services regularly. Because she was illiterate her memory was keen. She remembered the Biblical teachings and became active in visitation. She prayed often for the sick and the Lord rewarded her faith with the gift of healing. Her life was so radiant that within three years her husband and two sons believed and were baptized.

The Lord also burdened Mrs. Chan for her unsaved family in Henglung. Whenever she could, she would travel the 220 kilometers home and face her mother, her brothers and her sisters with the Gospel. Her youngest brother, Yeh Lien Ting, was the head of the district of Chung Ko. His duties made it necessary to attend many feasts and he became a heavy drinker. The drinking led to severe liver damage. Mrs. Chan decided to put her faith in God on the line. She faced her brother and said: "I will pray that the Lord will take away your desire for liquor and heal your body." The Lord heard her prayers and it was evident to Mr. Yeh that his sister's God was powerful.

After Mr. Yeh was healed, he agreed to having his sister invite a preacher into the home. Early the following day, Mrs. Chan set out for Tungshih. It was seven in the morning when she appeared at the Johansen home in Tungshih asking for someone to go with her to preach to her family right away. Since Rev. Johansen wasn't home, a fellow missionary went with Mrs. Chan to get acquainted and say that arrangements for regular services would be made when Rev. Johansen returned.

Rev. Johan Johansen is a second generation missionary of the Evangelical Lutheran Free Church of Norway. He spoke good Mandarin at the time he began the ministry in Henglung. His wife is a medical doctor and has a clinic in front of their home next to the church. They also operate a Chinese kindergarten.

In mid-May 1968, when regular services were begun in Henglung, Miss Chou from Miaoli was the kindergarten teacher. She was a graduate of the Hsinchu Bible School and spoke Hakka since she was raised in Miaoli. Her father was a Presbyterian elder who had been active in Hakka evangelism in the Miaoli area in the 1960's. Miss Chou interpreted for Rev. Johansen into the Hakka dialect.

Soon after the beginning of the Henglung ministry, Mr. Lai Chin Fu was also hired to help. At that time he was in college at Chung Hsing University in Taichung. Before college he had pastored a Finnish Free Church in Hou Lung, Miaoli County. He was the only Christian in his Hakka family in Tunglo and had a burden to reach his people. He translated choruses and hymns into Hakka and usually led the services. Over a period of years he has worked on a hymnal which has finally been mimeographed and is now used in all of the

fellowships. Mr. Lai lives with his wife and three sons in Houli,
Taichung County. He is now a teacher in a Jr. High School in San Yi,
Miaoli County.

Mrs. Chan had already taught the older women to pray and some
had experienced answers to their prayers. They, therefore, were
the most responsive to the Gospel. During one discussion time someone asked what Christians do about ancestor worship. Rev. Johansen
wasn't prepared for the question so he hesitated. Before he was
ready to answer, the wife of the oldest brother said: "In all these
years that I offered food to our ancestors they have not taken what
I offered nor have they done anything for me." That ended the discussion on ancestor worship and it has not been raised since.

In May, 1969, after a year of services in Henglung, Mrs. Chan
came to Rev. Johansen before the service and said: "Pastor, tonight
you must speak about baptism." Then after the message that night
Mrs. Chan stood up and came forward to conduct a very lively and personal invitational meeting. After twenty-six raised their hands,
Mrs. Chan asked Rev. Johansen to baptize the group. Rev. Johansen
persuaded Mrs. Chan to give him a few weeks to instruct them for baptism.

During the three weeks before the baptism, Rev. Johansen and Miss
Chou spent many hours carefully instructing the candidates. The oldest brother had felt pressured by his sister and decided against baptism. He also refused to let his family be baptized. His wife was
very hurt because she was among the most fervent of the believers.

At the service three weeks later, eighteen followed the Lord in
baptism. Those baptized included the second brother's widow; the
third brother, his wife, his three sons and a daughter-in-law; the
fourth brother (district head), his wife, two sons and daughter; old
Mother Yeh; three relatives and two friends.

In Feb., 1970, Mother Yeh passed away just as though she had
fallen asleep. Her peaceful passing at 94 years of age was a wonderful testimony to the whole community. As befitting the mother of
the district head, the funeral was big and attended by many digni-
taries.

Mrs. Chan made sure no non-Christian element got into the service.
When a musical group came to express their sorrow with traditional
music, Mrs. Chan stopped them. Rev. Johansen asked the district head

the meaning of the group's coming to play. He said it was to express
their sorrow and to pay respects. Rev. Johansen got Mrs. Chan's per-
mission for the group to play before the service started and Mr. Yeh
happily ran to bring the group back to have them perform.

Other functional substitutes agreed to by Mrs. Chan included:
1. A tiered stand behind the casket with rows of real and artificial
flowers and a picture of Mother Yeh at the center of the top row. A
cloth banner above the stand read "Enjoying Eternal Rest." The stand
had a canopy over it and black banners with a white cross and white
lettering hung on either side. 2. The casket was draped with a
black cloth with a white cross and four characters reading: "Retiring
to the heavenly home with glory." 3. Family members had white cotton
robes and head dresses and the immediate family stayed by the casket
until the service began. 4. Attending Christians wore a white cotton
band diagonally across their chest. 5. A large flower cross stood
in front of the casket and other floral memorials were placed on either side. 6. Those giving eulogies were encouraged to face the audience instead of the casket. 7. A uniformed band played several numbers as a part of the service and marched in the procession to the
grave. 8. The casket was carefully lined up to directional markers
at each end of the grave.

After the funeral Rev. Johansen very wisely decided to hold a
weekly remembrance service in the Yeh home. The weekly service was
continued for seven weeks with the seventh week being a special time
of food and fellowship. These meetings served both as an excellent
opportunity to explain the Biblical teachings on life and death and
to show unbelievers that Christians do remember and honor their ancestors. A further benefit of the services was that they satisfied
the desire for the relatives to do something instead of the heathen
seven week memorials.

The district head has been considered the de facto chairman of
the group in Henglung. He usually officiates in taking the offering
and speaks for the group. Other business matters are discussed with
adults or older young people, but there is no formal organization
of the group. The offerings are used for relief purposes and some
are given in appreciation to Mr. Lai. They have no budget and seem
to have little interest in either setting aside a special room for
services or building specifically for the purpose.

There has been little in a connected series of teaching besides
the instruction for baptism. The preaching is done by Mr. Lai, who
usually also leads the service, Rev. Johansen or a visiting speaker.

There was only one baptism in Dec. 1969, but 17 were baptized
at Easter, 1970, and one more at Christmas the same year. The following year (June 1971 to Aug. 1972) Rev. & Mrs. Johansen were on
furlough and there were no baptisms. (See graph) It appears that
the impetus for continued outreach depends on Rev. Johansen. When
he came back from furlough, he started studying the Tungshih accent
of the Hakka dialect. His year of study also shows its effect on
the ministry. (See graph) During the year of study only four were
baptized - two at Christmas, 1972 and two at Easter, 1973. Rev.
Johansen is dedicated to the evangelism of the Hakka, but it appears
that he has not been able to pass the torch to the Hakka.

The ministry in Henglung has become quite static. The early attendance of almost forty gradually decreased to about twenty in 1972
after the meetings started in Chungko (see below) and the young people began going into the military, marrying and going into business.
Because the Yeh home is in the country, the neighbors are scattered.
Outreach to new people would mean walking a kilometer or two over
hilly dirt roads in the dark. It appears that the original Hakka
Home Fellowship may be limited to the Yeh family and a few immediate
neighbors.

OUTREACH

1. Tamopu. During the days preceding the funeral of Mother
Yeh, February 1970, Mrs. Chan stayed with her youngest sister in
Tamaopu, a farming village a few kilometers east of Tungshih. She
encouraged Mrs. Chang to open her home to the preaching of the Gospel
just as their brother had done in Henglung. Mrs. Chang finally agreed,
so on Easter, 1970, the second Hakka Home Fellowship was begun.

In the beginning the meetings were held in three homes on a rotating basis. However, only a few months later, old Mr. Liu passed
away. He was the grandfather in one of the homes in which the group
had met. No one told Rev. Johansen of the passing so proper respects
and memorials could not be made. From that time on the Liu home was
closed to the Fellowship and the two Liu brothers and the widow of
the oldest stopped attending the services which were held in the

Chang home thereafter.

On Christmas, 1970 there were four from Tamopu who followed the Lord in baptism: Mrs. Chang and her son, her husband's brother-in-law (a mainlander who speaks Hakka) and a neighbor lady. Mr. Chang said he had no objection to his wife's baptism; however, when his older daughter wanted to be baptized, he objected because it would narrow down her prospects for a husband to Christians only. In March, 1971, Mrs. Chang's younger daughter was baptized too. There have been no baptisms since.

The attendance at the Sunday evening service has been about the same from the time it was held only in the Chang home. There are about ten adults and as many young people or children who attend quite regularly. The group of five baptized believers has no

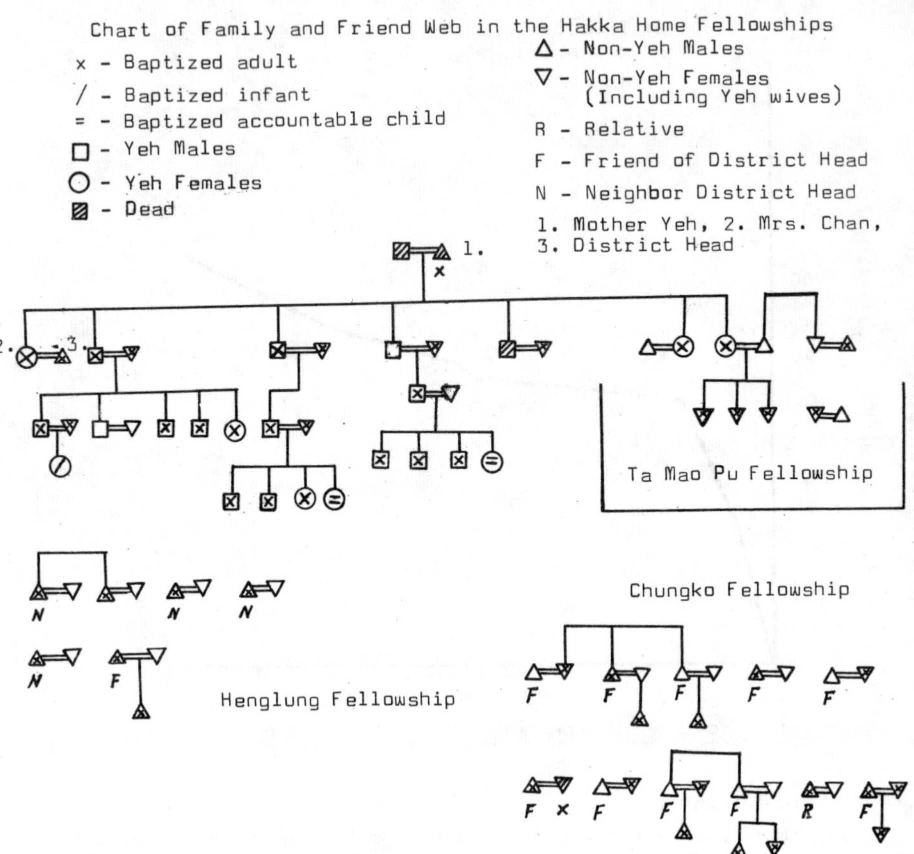

organization. There are no Hakka heads of households nor complete
families. The service is conducted by paid Christian workers. The
preaching is done by the Christian worker, a missionary or a guest
speaker. This group has not had the foundation in teaching which
the Henglung group had both from Mrs. Chan's visits before 1968
and the twice weekly services Rev. Johansen held in Henglung in
1968 and 1969. Neither has there been the testimony of a funeral
like that for Mother Yeh. Everything is done by the missionary or
Christian worker and the audience is the passive receiver.

A bright spot in the work at Tamaopu is the Sunday School and

Young People's ministries. Mrs. Chang as well as the children are
active in inviting outsiders to Sunday School, so the attendance
runs between fifty and sixty. Many of the children also come to
the worship service.

There are two Young People's groups meeting in the Chang home.
One was started early in 1976 by Mr. Chiang Mao Sung, a student at
Central Taiwan Theological College at the time. (Since his graduation from college in June, 1976, he has been responsible for the
ministry at Tamaopu. He is a paid worker.) The group meets on
Saturday evenings and has an attendance of between fifteen and
twenty. The other Young People's group was started in late September,
1976, by a Christian teacher in the Tamaopu middle school. She invited Miss Lin Ming Chu (See below) to help and they minister together to these Young People. The meeting is on Tuesday evening
with about ten to fifteen girls. (Miss Lin Ming Chu has been a
full-time paid Christian worker since her graduation from Central
Taiwan Theological Collége in June, 1976. She is a Hakka girl from
Chutung.)

2. Chungko. A week or two after Easter, 1970, Rev. Johansen
and Mr. Lai began services at Chungko, the small farming village
between Tungshih and Henglung. Mr. Yeh Lien Ting had his office
there as district head. Some from Chungko have ridden with Rev.
Johansen to Henglung for the weekly services almost from the beginning. One of those baptized in June, 1969 was from Chungko.

The services in Chungko were begun in Mr. Yeh's office. They
averaged about fifteen adults in the beginning. Not much later,
five of them declared their desire to be baptized. In the joint
baptismal service at the Norwegian Evangelical Lutheran Free Church
in Tungshih on Christmas, 1970, they were baptized. With old Mr.
Tai who had been baptized in Henglung, the Chungko group now had
six baptized believers.

As Mr. Yeh's office building deteriorated, the group began meeting in three homes on a rotating basis in early 1972. After six
months the group met regularly in a widow's home. However, the
widow was very fastidious and her house was small and stuffy and
the attendance soon dropped to about eight.

One of the homes where services had been held on a rotating
basis was the Chang Pi T'ung home. Mr. Chang was an examiner and

writer of legal documents. When Mrs. Johansen found that Mrs. Chang
had cancer, she sent her to Puli Christian Hospital for an operation.
Mrs. Chang was quite well for a while and was baptized with her husband's aunt in Dec., 1972. The following year Mrs. Chang's condition
worsened so her brother in Japan had her go there for treatment. Her
husband attended the meetings regularly while she was gone. The
treatment in Japan didn't help much and when she returned her condition deteriorated steadily. In the spring of 1975 the meetings were
held in the Chang home. Mrs. Chang was very patient and a witness
to her family and neighbors; on June 6, 1975, she passed away. The
funeral and the seven weekly meetings following were an effective
testimony to the neighborhood. Mr. Chang soon trusted the Lord and
was baptized at Christmas, 1975, with five others from Chungko.

A month after Mrs. Chang's passing, Mr. Chang invited the group
to meet in his home. Almost immediately the group doubled in size.
They are now talking of finding a piece of land and of building a
place for worship. Mr. Chang and other men participate in leading
the meeting and praying but all the preaching is done by the missionary, a Christian worker paid by the mission or a guest speaker.
There is no formal organization in Chungko, but this fellowship holds
the best promise of continuing growth.

Inter-group Fellowship

Fellowship has been a big part in the ministries from the beginning. Usually there is a time of visiting before the service starts
and after the service closes. The two big times of fellowship each
year when all three groups gather together are at Easter and Christmas. Either a supper or refreshments is part of the festal gathering.
It is at these times that baptisms are performed. The services have
usually been held at the Lutheran Church in Tungshih and a guest
speaker addresses the group.

Most recently (Fall 1976) the group of Lutheran Churches, affil-
iated with the Evangelical Lutheran Free Church of Norway, have tried
to make the Hakka Home Fellowships part of their organization, but
they have been rebuffed by the Fellowships. Their affiliation is
directly with the missionary and there is no organizational liaison.

Missionary Reinforcements

In the fall of 1972 Rev. Einar Braadland of the Taiwan Lutheran
Missionary Association began working with Rev. Johansen. He studied
the Tungshih accent of the Hakka dialect and now helps with the
preaching.

Weaknesses

The greatest weakness in the Hakka Home Fellowships is the lack
of lay training both in Biblical truths as well as in outreach evangelism. A lay person was responsible for the beginning of the ministry but the people have been mostly preached at rather than taught
precept upon precept. Furthermore, the missionary has not planned
for lay leadership. He has rather hired Christian workers as he sees
the need and hopes that the Fellowships will eventually take on the
salaries.

The second weakness follows on the footsteps of the first. Because the people aren't trained, they have little understanding of
their purpose as a "Fellowship." They don't have to pay a preacher
or rent a building so there is no pressure to get more people to
help or more money to cover expenses. Because the people don't know
how to witness, they depend on people's coming to the service to hear
the Gospel. They are not vocal witnesses of God's grace wherever
they go and in whatever they do.

Suggestions

The small fellowship groups with the informality of the home could
be an excellent setting for a thorough training program. Then as
truths are learned, the group could be taken to another place to put
into practice what has been learned. There is a big need for the
believers to be involved with the missionary in an outreach to other
places.

Contiguous with training is the necessity to involve the Christians in the planning for the continued spiritual growth of the group
and outreach to new people and places. Certain individuals can be
suggested or appointed for various aspects of the program. As much
as possible help them to feel that the program is theirs and that
it will succeed or fail depending on each one's faithfulness to his
or her responsibility.

ABOUT THE AUTHOR

Ernest Boehr is a second generation missionary to China. He
took his college work in Science and Bible at Wheaton College and
had two years of graduate work in Christian Education at Columbia
Bible College. He went as a missionary to Taiwan with the Evangelical Alliance Mission in 1954 learning first the Mandarin and then
the Hakka dialect of Chinese. During two furloughs in California he
studied Psychology at Fuller Theological Seminary and then took
studies in Church Growth at the Fuller School of World Mission. He
is presently putting the Gospel into colloquial Chinese.

Chapter 3

THE CHUKUANG FREE METHODIST CHURCH STORY--A FAITH
EXPERIMENT IN CHURCH GROWTH

One effective way to experience church growth within the Taiwan
harvest field is to utilize the church planting potential of young
maturing churches. A host of churches planted in post-war years are
reaching maturity and are looking for new avenues of service and
witness. Other younger, growing churches, nearing maturity, are
making plans for further progress. A number of these congregations
have already launched out into responsive unevangelized, or sparsely
evangelized areas, with the definite purpose of planting a new church,
and they have witnessed favorable success. Therefore, the principle
being set forth in this study of the Chukuang Church is that healthy
growth will take place when alert church leaders and lay workers
of young maturing churches locate receptive areas of population, and,
with vision, faith and planning, move forward in church planting
endeavors. Furthermore, the newly planted churches in Taiwan's
present socio-economic structure have the potential to mature quickly
as indigenous churches. This type of action takes positive steps
to fulfill the demands of Christ's Great Commission. This all important commission to reproduce must be taken seriously. If not,
manpower and money will be channelled off for the "many good things"
at the sacrifice of the best.

The church under study is one of the twenty-eight churches within
the Taiwan Free Methodist Church Annual Conference, and it is the
result of a young maturing church's reaching out with the definite
purpose of planting a new church. It is like a mother-daughter re-
lationship--the mother church produces a daughter church.

The Chukuang Church is located in Chukuang Village which is in
the Tsoying district of the city of Kaohsiung. It is one mile north

43

of the large Chinese Naval Base Complex, one mile south of the large
Nantse Export Processing Zone, and it borders the Kaohsiung Oil Refinery to the east. The village is a new housing settlement made
up of two story apartments. These apartments are built in long rows,
with some rows having as many as 50 homes. On the main streets the
majority of the apartments have been constructed for storefront businesses.

In 1972 when the Chukuang Church sprang into being, the village
had some 1500 homes with a population of about 6000. In two years
of continual, large scale construction, there were 3000 homes. A
population of 15,000 was anticipated. The church has a good location
in the central area of the village.

The population is composed of both Mandarin-speaking and Taiwanese-speaking Chinese. The majority of the first apartments were
bought or rented by navy personnel. The other apartments have been
bought or rented by merchants and workmen of various trades and companies. The families may be classified within the middle and lower
middle socio-economic levels.

The church is actually composed of two homogeneous groups. One
half of the membership is Mandarin-speaking Chinese and one half is
Taiwanese-speaking. The majority of the latter also speak Mandarin.
Although the majority of the members meet together for the Sunday
morning Mandarin Chinese service, a second service is conducted in
the afternoon to accommodate those who do not understand Mandarin.
A number of the Mandarin and Taiwanese-speaking members attend both
services.

There are a number of special features and reasons why this church
merits our attention.

First, the Chukuang Church is a granddaughter church, or some
might wish to call it a third generation church. It is an example
of what can be done by the continuous outreach of young churches.

Second, within two years the church was fully organized and
fully self-supporting. This indicates that young churches have the
potential to organize and support their church programs very quickly.

Third, the study of the church strongly suggests there are many
responsive areas for church planting ministries in Taiwan's drastically
changing society, especially because of the phenomenal increase in
urban populations. Furthermore, the study points out the necessity
of locating these receptive areas.

Fourth, the leading participants in the Chukuang Church planting project were ordinary Christians, both adults and young people, who, under the leadership of their alert pastor went forth in faith, trusting the Holy Spirit to work through them. Here is an example of vision, prayer, faith, planning and boldly going forth in the power of Christ.

Fifth, the study indicates that the planting church (mother church) was strengthened and blessed by God as a result of launching out in faith.

Sixth, the church began in a Christian's home, moved to a rented storefront, and then moved to a two apartment structure which was located at the end of a long row of apartment buildings. During construction the two apartments were built so that the first floor could serve as the sanctuary and the second floor as the pastor's residence.

Seventh, the church is still growing and is developing the potential that could in the near future move forward and plant a fourth generation church (great-granddaughter).

Eighth, the church has tried to accommodate the Mandarin and Taiwanese-speaking Chinese by conducting separate services for them.

For an adequate description of the Chukuang Church, we must go back to the first generation church. A historical survey informs us that only 18 years passed between the planting of the first and third churches, and as of 1975, the three churches have gathered a total communicant membership of 359.

The first generation church, or the grandmother of the Chukuang Church, is the Kaohsiung Ho Ping Hsiang Free Methodist Church. This congregation came into being in 1954 and was one of the first churches planted by the Free Methodist Mission in Taiwan. By 1955, a plain, large church building was dedicated. The funds for the structure were contributed by the Free Methodist Mission Board. When this Kaohsiung church ventured out in 1964 to plant a new church, her communicant membership was 112 and there were 38 preparatory members. Total offerings for that year amounted to U.S.$1,258.

This congregation, stimulated by its pastor, resolved to reach out with the Gospel to the people in a large Chinese Naval Housing Area four miles away. This housing area, Kuomao Village, is located in the Tsoyine district of Kaohsiung City. The village has some

2900 homes with a population of about 15,000. The first services
were held in a home, then in a storefront building, later in a
temporary structure, and finally in the present Kuomao Church building-
ing.

The move was spearheaded by a very zealous and evangelistic-
minded pastor. Although he was totally blind physically, he had
keen vision spiritually. A number of earnest lay Christians and
students from the Holy Light Theological College joined with the
pastor. This daughter church, Kuomao, experienced excellent growth.
By the end of 1975 the communicant membership stood at 179 and there
were 7 preparatory members. Total church offerings amounted to
U.S.$7,638. We might add here that the Kuomao Church building, land,
and pastor's residence (U.S.$11,500) were financed by a generous con-
tribution from the Free Methodist Mission Board, Chinese Christians
and from foreign missionaries.

A most interesting and exciting fact is that this Kuomao daughter
herself has now launched out and planted a daughter church - the
Chukuang Church of this study. The Kuomao Church proves that even
young Christians can successfully win others to Christ. In May 1973,
the Kumao Church pastor and Christians were challenged by the Chukuang
new apartment area just two miles away. As mentioned above, it was
anticipated that a population of 15,000 would soon fill the village.

This church planting was undertaken by the zealous pastor, Tsang
Teng-yin, adult lay workers (men and women), young people from the
church youth group, students from the Holy Light Theological College,
and two missionaries (the latter giving only a small amount of time
to the project).

Again, the results were striking as we indicated in the introduction. In just two years this granddaughter Chukuang Church was
fully self-supporting, had 60 communicant members, 10 preparatory
members and a Sunday School attendance of 80. Later statistics
(December 1975) recorded 80 communicant members, 15 preparatory members, an average Sunday School attendance of 60, a youth group of
30 and a women's group of 25. The total church offerings for 1975
were N.T. 140,973.40 (U.S. $3,710.).

The Kuomao mother church negotiated a ten year loan of U.S.
$7000 from the Free Methodist Mission Board and purchased two apart-
ment buildings under construction. They were to be used as a

sanctuary and pastor's residence. The church also received gifts
from many Chinese Christians and a few foreign missionaries.

Therefore, in this brief historical sketch we have an excellent
example of good extension growth. This growth is described graphically
in figure one. Please note, also, that as this extension growth took
place by national Christians, the shape of the church buildings became more indigenous (more practical and suitable for Chinese society
than most European and American church edifices).

FIGURE ONE

EXTENSION GROWTH OF TWO RECENTLY MATURING CHURCHES

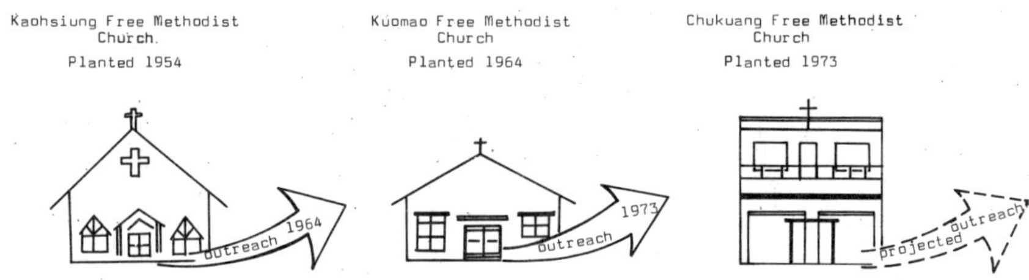

In order to become better acquainted with the inner workings of
God and men in the church planting and the growth that followed, it
will be helpful to note the dynamics of the three year growth pattern
and the projected growth for 1976. Note the results of a survey conducted in 1974 on the nature of the new congregation; note the resources and strength that brought success and examine the methods
which were used.

The pattern of growth is shown on a straight line, vertical type
graph. This shows the rise in growth each year (see figure 2). It
also indicates by a broken line the projected growth for 1976.

In October, 1974, the writer conducted a survey among the communicant members (those baptized and having full church membership
status) to gain a knowledge of the age and sex distribution of the
new congregation, the birthplace of members and the source of membership. The results showed that 75% of the communicant members ranged
from 20 years to 65 years of age. Twenty-five percent were under
20 years old. As to occupational background, there are Chinese

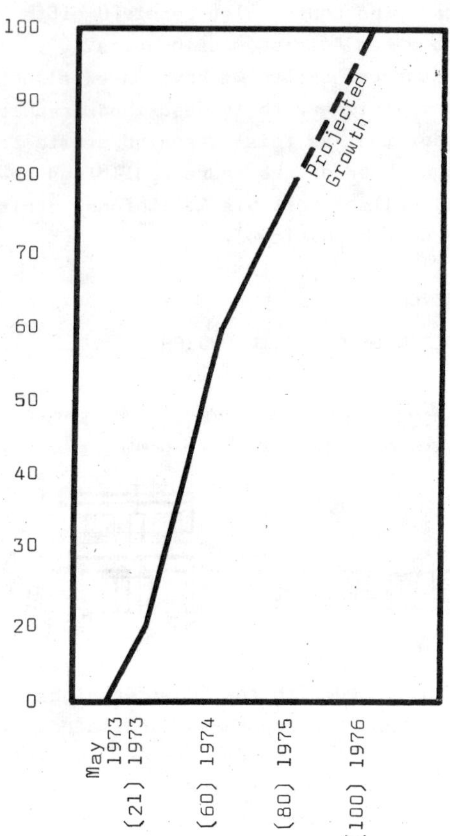

FIGURE TWO
CHUKUANG CHURCH
PATTERN
OF
GROWTH

Navy personnel, workers at the Oil Refinery and Nantze Export Processing Zone. A few members are in small businesses. There were
more female members than male--two to one. Fifty percent of the
members were born on the Mainland of China and 50 percent were born
in Taiwan. Fifty-five percent of the members were converted and
baptized by the Chukuang Church and forty-five percent transferred
into the church from other churches. By 1975 there were 23 whole
family units within the church membership. In the majority of these
families the husband is from the Mainland and the wife is from Taiwan.
These results may be seen graphically in figure 3.

<u>Figure Three</u>

Nature of the Church Presented Graphically

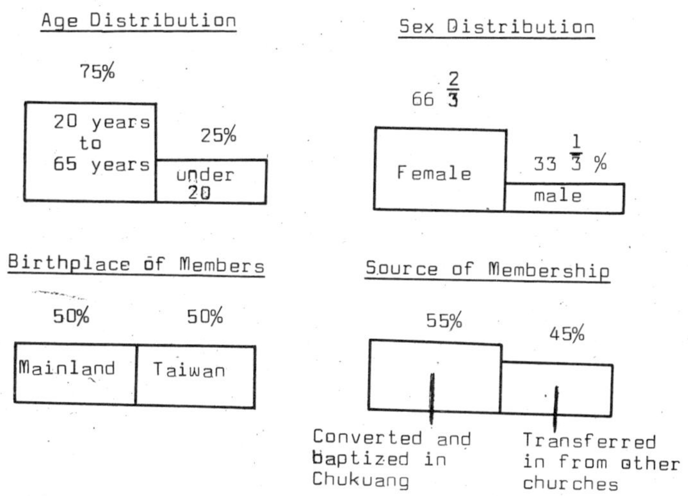

It is well to note here that when the church planting project began in Chukuang there wasn't any organized church in the village. There was a home meeting in the home of a Peniel Church member. This meeting was later discontinued. The Conservative Baptist Mission began a church planting project there in 1974. However, this work was discontinued in 1975. The story of the problems involved and the closing of the project is written in the May, 1975 issue of the <u>Taiwan Church Growth Bulletin</u> Vol. III. No.2, page 2. The Presbyterians have recently come into the village and opened a chapel. However, this seems to be mainly for Presbyterians who have moved into the village, and so far the congregation is less than twenty-five. In relation to these reports, we must mention a few problems that confronted the new Chukuang Free Methodist Church.

During the beginning of the church planting ministry the problem of identity was experienced. Who were these people renting this storefront building? What is their purpose? What are they teaching? At first, church attendance was irregular. There was inadequate

49

calling as the busy pastor of the mother church and the laity had
only limited time to give. These problems, however, were overcome
when a student pastor, his wife and family moved to Chukuang Village
and settled in a rented home near the chapel.

It is possible to summarize the resources and strengths that
brought success under three main topics: Personnel, Financial and
Spiritual.

Personnel

1. The active, alert, and talented leadership of the Kuomao Church
pastor, Rev. Tsang Teng-yin, led the church planting project and
carefully shepherded the new congregation until a full-time pastor
was appointed to the Chukuang Church. Even then he continued to ad-
vise. His talented wife also gave valuable aid. Both are seminary
graduates.
2. A group of earnest, alert and active laymen and laywomen, of
whom only a few had training in evangelistic outreach, gave valuable
aid.
3. An energetic youth group and women's group gave aid.
4. An energetic overseas Chinese lady from the Philippines also
helped.
5. Students from the Holy Light Theological College, and one, Hsiung
Lung-hsing, who was later appointed to the Chukuang Church to serve
as full time pastor were important to the success of the project.
His good wife, Mrs. Hsiung, became a tremendous soul winner and was
indispensible to the success of the work.
6. Two missionaries helped part time at the invitation of the Kuomao
Church. One missionary continued working with the new congregation,
leading a one year's Bible study and preaching once a month.

Financial

1. Good church offerings at the mother (Kuomao) church were added
to other good offerings that began coming to the newly planted church.
2. Special gifts were given to the Kuomao Church for its church
planting ministry from interested Christians. Once the new church
was on its way, interested Christians also gave to the Chukuang
Church.
3. The willingness of the Free Methodist Mission Board to negotiate
a loan for the mother church so that a permanent church structure
could be purchased was necessary for success.

1. The strong, spiritual leadership of Pastor (Rev.) Tsang Teng-yin and his wife were invaluable. Besides the evangelistic emphasis in the pastor's ministry, Mrs. Tsang's fine musical program in the church added greatly to the church planting.

2. The fresh, energizing zeal of new, active adult Christians who were anxious to witness and share their new found faith assured success.

3. A spiritually-minded women's group in the mother church added valuable prayer support. Some ladies were able to give time for Sunday School teaching and house-to-nouse calling. This group included a Mrs. Chang, an 85 year old overseas Japanese woman, who has lived in Taiwan for over 30 years. She is gifted in prayer and faith and has offered valuable prayer intercession for the new church planting ministry and for the new Chukuang congregation. Even now she is invited to speak to the Chukuang group.

4. Early morning prayer meetings were conducted at the mother church. These were also begun in the new church.

5. A fine group of evangelistic-minded young people from the mother church took part in special meetings and other activities connected with the new work.

6. The encouragement and prayer support of missionaries and many interested Christians from other Free Methodist Churches were of great help.

7. The miraculous healings of two children in two Chukuang Church member's homes drew interest. The testimony of the parents of the children who were healed brought new converts into the church.

We will discover, that the methods used in the church planting ministry were not extraordinary. They were actually simple, but varied. The methods used were fitted to a responsive segment of population. By receptivity, we are referring to people who came from Mainland China and were especially open to the Gospel. Many had left members of their families on the Mainland. Many had become disenchanted with the helpless religious practices of the past and were open to the Gospel message of hope. We also refer to the local Taiwanese people who formerly were strongly influenced by practices of the Buddhist religion including practices of kinship ritual and various traditional superstitions. Now having moved into the city they are free to

investigate the Christian religion. There is frustration and loneli-
ness in the city areas as these people are caught in rapid social
change. They can find fellowship within the Christian community.

These simple methods drew from the resources, strengths and
spiritual gifts of laymen and laywomen. The laity of our Taiwan
churches are able to provide financially for church planting. They
can also open their homes for house churches, home Bible studies,
and children's meetings. There are treasure houses of natural tal-
ents among our lay members that can be used for the Kingdom of God.
Most important are the spiritual gifts which God gives to all his
people for the advance and growth of the Church. There are over
twenty specific spiritual gifts mentioned in the New Testament (see
Romans 12:3-8; I Corinthians 12:1-11, 28-31; Ephesians 4:11-13;
I Peter 4:9, 10; I Corinthians 7:7; 13:3). The majority of these
gifts are found among the laity. These are generally never realized,
understood or used until an open door is given for the exercising
of them.

These methods also drew from the resources of Heaven, God's
grace and power. God answered the prayers and faith of these earnest
Christian workers. He gave the power to witness; His Spirit worked
in the hearts of the non-believers, and He brought in the harvest
through the efforts of concerned Christians.
1. This is how the church planting in Chukuang progressed. On May
21, 1973 the first service was held in the home of Mr. and Mrs. Teng.
The Tengs were Kuomao Church members who had moved to Chukuang to
live. They invited other Christians in the village to attend. The
meeting was led by the Kuomao pastor. Also in attendance were the
two missionaries that the Kuomao Church had invited. There was prayer
a short message, and discussion on how to proceed with plans. Brief
plans were outlined.
2. Home meetings were held each Sunday. Within a month's time a
storefront building was rented for a chapel. Gifts immediately
came in to help pay the rent, purchase chairs, Bibles, song books,
blackboard, signs, etc. The Tengs, who lived near the chapel, gave
valuable assistance in the preparing of the chapel for services each
morning and evening of the scheduled program.
3. On Sunday afternoons, Sunday School was held from 3:00 to 4:00.
The first teachers were laywomen and young people from the mother

church. One, who took heavy responsibility, was a former teacher
in a school of nursing. At first a missionary supplied teaching
materials, but later the new congregation (with some gifts to help)
bought their own materials.
4. The weekly worship service was held immediately following the
Sunday School hour, from 4:00 to 5:00. Rev. Tsang spoke or invited
guest speakers. At times he invited various lay workers to come
and give their testimonies.
5. English classes were held on Wednesday evenings. At first,
three classes were conducted. Later only two classes were needed.
Bible study was a part of each English class. After the new church
was organized, the English classes were dropped completely and the
missionary teacher took over the Mandarin Bible Study in the new
church.
6. Schedules of the times of the church services were printed. On
Sunday afternoons before the worship service, the pastor, young people, and some adult lay workers went from door-to-door inviting people to attend the services. The schedule card and a Gospel tract
were left in the homes.
7. Special evangelistic efforts included:
    (a) A team of young people from the States who conducted a
        special children's evangelistic service.
    (b) In August, two evenings of outdoor film evangelism were
        provided. The chapel was used and the vacant lot next
        door to it. These meetings drew crowds of 150 and 250
        people. A literature van was parked nearby filled with
        Bibles and Christian books. The Kuomao women's group
        came and gave a special number in song one evening, and
        the youth group came the second evening. They also wit-
        nessed for Christ by their singing.
8. In September, a youth service was organized and scheduled on
Saturday evenings. At times the Kuomao youth group rode their bi-
cycles to the chapel to join the new youth services. This was an
encouragement to new Christians.
9. In September, three students from Holy Light Theological College
were appointed to help in the new church. They called from house-
to-house on Saturdays, conducted the youth services, taught Sunday
School classes, and helped in the worship services.

10. Beginning the first week in October, the worship services were
changed from the afternoon to morning. Rev. Tsang spoke once a month,
two missionaries once a month, and a student or guest speaker once a
month.

11. On Sunday afternoon Rev. Tsang conducted an instruction class
for people desiring baptism and preparatory membership. These people were taken in as full communicant members soon after their baptism.

12. Soon after this the Taiwan Free Methodist Annual Conference appointed a student from Holy Light Theological College to serve as
pastor. Student Hsiung Lung-hsing, his wife and family moved to
Chukuang and lived in rented quarters near the chapel. Pastor Hsiung
is still the pastor. He and his wife have made a very valuable contribution to the Chukuang success. Both are gifted in personal evangelism. Pastor Hsiung, a Mainlander, has good rapport with those
from the Mainland and also with the Taiwanese. He has become fluent
in speaking Taiwanese and preaches in the afternoon Taiwanese service
which was added to the program after the permanent church building
was purchased. Mrs. Hsiung, a Taiwanese, has excellent rapport with
the Taiwanese ladies. She and her husband have led most of them to
Christ in personal work. After Pastor Hsiung's graduation from Seminary in June, 1974, he took full time pastoral responsibilities.

13. When the chapel was packed full, plans were made to purchase
a permanent church building. Arrangements were made with a building
contractor to buy two of his apartment buildings which were side by
side. Since the contractor had not yet built the structures, instruc-
tions were given to construct the two buildings for a church building,
with the pastor's residence on the second floor. This is when the
mother church negotiated a loan from the Free Methodist Mission Board.

14. The dedication service for the new Chukuang Church was conducted
in December of 1973.

15. Along with the regular weekly services, Sunday evening home
meetings have become very popular in various sections of the village.
This is an additional way to reach non-Christians.

16. It is the hope of the writer that this church will continue to
grow and reach out soon with extension growth and plant a daughter
church. If this does take place, we will have a great-granddaughter
church.

Chukuang Church

What would have been two apartments has been constructed into a church (Pastor Hsiung Lung-hsing and wife standing outside)

Eleven baptized - September 1976 (Pastor Hsiung seated on the right)

Twelve baptized on January 2, 1977

In summary, the mother-daughter church planting method has great
possibilities in Taiwan today. It is natural and healthy. It gives
Christians an opportunity to exercise their spiritual gifts and feel
blessed of God in doing their part to win the nations to Christ.
They experience joy in winning their own people. We can also say
that winning souls for Christ keeps the devil away. The fires of
God keep burning in the heart of the church planter. Fulfilling
the Great Commission develops a spiritual Christian. He knows what
victorious Christian living means. He is perfected to Christ-like
quality. A church, therefore, becomes filled with "quality Christians."

This method produces indigenousness. It concentrates on receptive
areas and observes the principle of the homogeneous unit. Christians
multiply churches in their own cultures and ethnic groups and Christianity loses its foreignness. The newly planted churches have local
color and practicality. Christian singing sounds more Chinese. Common linguistic ties and cultural likes attract and draw the non-
Christians to salvation and Christian fellowship.

Every church should consider church planting a top priority.
Every mature church has the potential to plant a new church. The
healthiest thing a church can do is to find a receptive area and
plant a daughter church.

ABOUT THE AUTHOR

Dorothy Raber was born into a Christian home near Canton, Ohio
on October 11, 1930.

She is an ordained minister in the Free Methodist Church and has
worked under the Free Methodist Mission in Taiwan since 1960. She has
been active in church planting ministries, and teaches New Testament,
Church Growth and Missiology at the Holy Light Theological College in
Kaohsiung.

She received her B.A. in Philosophy-Religion from Greenville
College, her B.D. and M.TH. from Asbury Theological Seminary and the
Doctor of Missiology from Fuller Theological Seminary.

TOK-HENG

PUT-
INTO-
PRACTICE-
CHURCH

The Tok-Heng Church

This is the story of a church which lives up to its name Tok-heng - "putting into practice" faith and making it attractive to others. It is a vibrant growing church. The consistent growth and outreach of this church has drawn it to our attention. Through interviews, obser-vations and study of the very limited church records, we have tried to construct a picture of the development of the church. One soon realizes that any analysis at best is only an observation of the mys-terious work of the Holy Spirit which John likens to the wind "it blows where it wills, and you hear the sound of it but you do not know whence it comes or whither it goes: so it is with anyone who is born of the spirit." Nevertheless, one may observe factors which have contributed to the birth, nurture and multiplication of Christians.

The Tok-heng church is located on the west side of the North District of Taichung off Wu Chuan and Ta Ya Road, on Tok-heng Road, Taichung City. One could say it is on the outer edge of the older section of Taichung City. The newer housing developments stretch many miles beyond its area to the north along Taya Road and to the west

toward Hsitun and Harbor Road. The church is located directly across
from the Second Provincial Boys' Middle School. It is a largely residential area with some small stores and businesses.

ECONOMIC MAKE UP

The members of the Tok-heng church are indigenous Taiwanese
with the exception of two brothers who are Mainland Chinese married
to Taiwanese Chinese. Most of the breadwinners are independent business men, office workers or laborers. There are two medical doctors,
six teachers and some craftsmen among the members. The majority would
fit into the lower-middle class. The church has a strong group of
middle-age and young members. The members live mostly in the immediate neighborhood of the church and are as a whole representative of
the population mosaic of the area. The area is an older, conservative
area and therefore does not experience the restlessness often associated with newer developments. It is a community with stability and
continuity.

A healthy plant needs trimming and can be split from the top
through the root and the smaller part planted in another place resulting in two beautiful healthy plants instead of one. This is how the
Tok-heng church was planted. In 1957 thirty members of the Liu Yuan
Presbyterian church agreed to leave their church and establish a Presbyterian churchlet, to be a Gospel center in the Tok-heng area where
they lived. This group consisted of twenty families with a potential
Christian community of eighty persons (the average size of a family
is considered to be four persons). From its inception the new church
was self-supporting. The church was under the leadership of the mother
church for one year. Since they had the required thirty members and
financial independence, the church was formally organized as a Presbyterian Church and Liau Un-ka was called to be full-time pastor-
evangelist.

On August 20, 1957, the church had thirty members. They bought
186 ping of land with an old house on it where worship services were
held. Later the house was extended in the front and to the sides and
modified into the sanctuary which is still in use today. Gradually
the church bought adjoining plots of land to meet the needs of the
growing church for Sunday School classrooms, parsonage and student
center - hostel. Presently the church owns 320 pings of land. A

58

new sanctuary is planned to replace the present structure which is
already inadequate for the overcrowded services and activities of the
church. A two story structure is projected with a basement to provide space for the programs. Tok-heng church was established not
only for the needs of its members in that place but also to be a center from which to launch out to other areas with the Gospel.

ORGANIZATION AND MEMBER INVOLVEMENT

The basic organization of the church is the Presbyterian pattern
of organization. The Annual membership meeting calls the pastor and
elects elders and deacons. The pastor works with the elders and deacons in carrying out the program of the church. All organizations
in the church are responsible to them. The church constituency is
divided into ten areas. Each area has two contact persons, an elder
or deacon assisted by one appointed person. Assigned jobs in the
church: Sunday School teachers, home worship leaders, ushers and the
flower arrangement committee, involve a large number of members throughout the year. This shows that the church expects its members to share
responsibilities in the church. It indicates that there are opportunities to gain experiences and to develop loyalty and love for the Lord
and His church. These shared responsibilities in the work of the
Lord by the members enhance church growth in depth and in numbers.

The members are not only active in the church program at home,
they are also encouraged to assist in evangelistic efforts in student
work and in various Gospel-church centers.

In studying the church organization and the assignment sheets
of the church, we have found the following analysis of member involvement:

1. Administrative: Church Council and Pastor   11
2. Organizations: Committee members for youth and
                    women's organizations, etc.   28
3. Service: Choir members   60
              Sunday School teachers, pianists, music
              conductor, area-contact persons   36
              Ushers, flower arrangement committee,
              leaders for home meetings, women's
              meeting and S. S. worship time
              (assigned for six month periods)   110

For the most part these assignments represent different people.
A few members have three or four responsibilities and some have two
responsibilities; however, as a whole, the assignments show a very
wide involvement of members:

PROGRAM

The church program follows mostly the traditional Presbyterian
pattern for Sunday School, worship services, Bible study and Home
Worship meetings; at the same time, it shows a creativity and an
adaptability to the congregation.

The Home Worship meetings are divided into Class A for adults
and Class B for young people. These Christian young people organize
and lead their own home worship. Rev. Lin attends these meetings on
a rotating basis.

The Tuesday evening Student meeting is for Christian students
and their friends from the Second Boys' Middle School located across
the street from the Tok-heng Church.

Special deeper life or revival services (Poe-leng hoe) are held
once a year around Easter time. The day before Christmas a special
evangelistic service is held.

The weekly church bulletin is utilized as a teaching instrument
as well as for announcements about the Sunday schedule, church events
and news. Special articles for youth and for adults, studies of Bible
books and doctrines, and studies in Christian life are included. After
several such studies, the pastor includes questions relating to the
articles for the congregation to answer. These questions are discussed
periodically following the morning worship service.

Rev. Lin is organizing a ten-disciple group composed of young
men and women seekers. This group is envisioned as an informal group
relating on different levels. The levels will include Christian
teaching in order to lead the seekers into a vital born-again relationship with Christ with all its implications for life and living.

While witnessing and evangelism are an integral part of the total
church program, the church is also projecting a more formal program
of "every member a witness." This program will help train believers
to gather in a greater harvest.

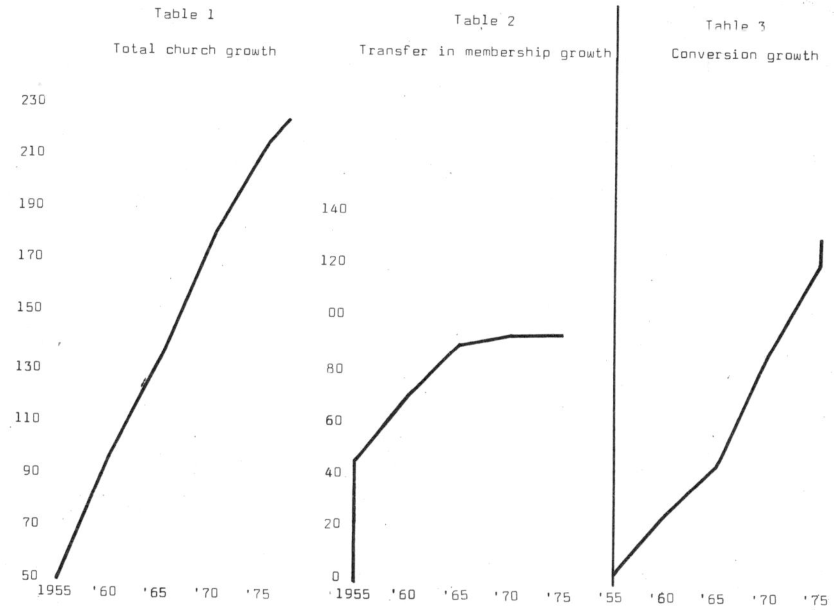

CHURCH GROWTH PATTERN

The Tok-heng church has experienced steady growth. (see Table I)
In analyzing the growth pattern of the church we found healthy growth
in each of the following areas.

a) Transfer growth. As already indicated the first members of
the church were transfers from a large Presbyterian church for the
purpose of establishing a church in this area. At present transfers
in and out balance each other. Members of other churches who are in
regular attendance here are listed as seekers until the transfer of
membership is completed. When membership is requested they are exam-
ined and accepted upon confession of faith before the congregation
after transfer procedures from the previous church to this church
have been completed. In recent years about sixty members have transferred out in order to help new churches and Gospel Centers in the
area of their residence. Five Gospel centers have been established
in this way. When the new church is organized, the membership is
transferred to the new church. Thus it seems there is a healthy attitude toward members who transfer out to help churches in their area

residence.

b) Biological growth. With a core of Christian families from
the beginning (twenty of the original families transferred are still
active in the church) there is also a continual element of biological
growth as these families continue to bring their children and grandchildren for baptism, salvation and confirmation. In the past two
years half of the thirty-four baptisms were from adults of Christian
families. Naturally as more Christian families are established and
conversions of complete family units take place, the reservoir for
biological growth in the church is sustained and increased.

c) Conversion growth. Members are often the bridges for the
conversion of other family members, relatives and friends. An elder
in the church cited a number of examples of this nature: A Christian
man passed away leaving a testimony that influenced his wife and children to become Christians; a son was saved and led his mother and others to the Lord; a business man failed in business and had no money
to offer sacrifices in the temple to change his bad fortune. A Christian invited him to share his problem with Christ. As a result, his
whole family accepted the Lord and that family has produced faithful
members in the Tok-heng church for years.

The records, as indicated in Table VII, show that transfer growth
and conversion growth were equal from 1955-1965. From 1965 till the
present the growth almost completely represents new member growth.
It is not always clear from the records whether the increase in membership is from Christian families (biological re-birth growth) or
from non-Christian families. In the past two years, one half of the
thirty believers baptized were from non-Christian backgrounds.

The records available for this study consisted of the membership
book which gives information about present members such as name, date
and place of baptism, age, sex, etc. From this information we have
constructed the graphs and tables. It should be noted, however, that
in the membership book it was not recorded who transferred to new congregations like the Hiong Siong church. If these transferred members
were baptized in the Tok-heng church, then the growth graph would show
considerably greater increase. There is no authoritative record of the
number of members who have helped establish new congregations in the
frame work of the larger Presbyterian outreach in the Taichung city
areas. Members recall that about thirty members went over from the

Tok-heng church to the Hiong Siong church and others went to other
new church beginnings, probably equaling a total of sixty members.

Taking into consideration that recent converts often have a fresh,
active expression of their faith and that they are often bridges to
the yet unconverted, it may be noted that twenty of the original members transferred to the Tok-heng church were recent converts. One may
also expect that they transferred loyalty to the new church more easily
than older members. It also appears that these newly converted, who
transferred to the newly established Tok-heng church, all lived in the
Tok-heng area. This fact helped facilitate such a move.

From Table IV we observe that transfer-in growth doubled in the
first decade of the church's existence; then it virtually stopped
while conversion growth increased steadily, tripling itself over the
second decade. It may be concluded that at the end of the first ten
years the transfer-in of members from other churches for the purpose of
supporting church growth was not needed and the church has done very
well in continuing and sustaining faster growth into the present.

From Table V it is interesting to note that in the A group the
number of male and female transfer-in members is practically equal.
This is also the case in the conversion growth bracket. At the same
time the totals of both the male and female members in the transfer-in
and conversion-growth sections are also about the same. This shows
good balance and gives stability as well as conditioning support to
faster church growth. The other categories in Table V speak for themselves and provide interesting fruit for thought, but they are not
too helpful in fostering church growth.

Table VI indicates that the number of seekers, including some
Christian visitors, is consistently at sixty persons for the Sunday
morning service. This shows a concrete group out of which converts
are constantly fed into the church.

The Sunday evening services have around fifty members in attendance.

One cannot study the growth of the Tok-heng church without considering the role in the planting of new churches in the Taichung area.
The church has vigorously supported this program with personnel and
funds from its beginning. The Hiong-Siong church was established in
this way. It is in a newer housing area. The church was begun in
1963 and was supported by members who lived there or who had moved

into the area. The church also benefited from the help of other
Presbyterian churches in Taichung. The Hiong Siong church is now
self-supporting and has one hundred twenty members. It has its own
spacious building and is independent of the Tok-heng church.

Other Gospel Centers have been established in various areas of
Taichung in cooperation with Taichung area Presbyterian churches.
Rev. Lin was in charge of the Chui-Lam church outreach for a while.
In March of this year, a pastor was secured for the church. Other
centers to which Tok-heng church members are related with support
are the Pak-Tun and the Hsai-Tun Presbyterian church beginnings.

The 1975 Tok-heng annual church financial report shows that
contributions toward the work of Taichung Gospel Centers was one and
one half times as much as the offerings for the building fund for the
projected larger building.

Tok-heng is dedicated to help these new churches with members as
well as funds. If members live in the area of the new church, their
membership is transferred when the new church is organized. The Tok-
heng church is to be commended for its vision and liberality in sharing
their funds and transplanting their members to grow new churches.

In talking to members of the church, one feels that they believe
in the church. They are successful in bringing people to Christ and
feel good about their members who spread out to bring little churches
into existence in other areas. They enjoy seeing them become big
churches. Dr. MacGavran used to say that if you want to have a lot
of big men you first have to have a lot of small boys. If you want a
lot of big churches you have to start with a lot of small ones.

What are the factors which contribute to the growth of the church?
Where does the finding, folding and feeding take place? There are
several observable factors which can be mentioned.

1. A strong preaching ministry. The worship services are an
experience of thanksgiving, adoring and glorifying God. There are
definite evangelistic and deeper life emphases. The relevance of the
message to the actual needs of the people listening makes Christ a
real option for the seeker and the source to meet the needs of the
believer and the seeker. The congregation gives rapt attention, and
one senses a spirit of celebration and of expectancy. Along with the
preaching ministry, the study material in the Sunday church bulletin
stimulates inquiry and growth. The questions become the focus of a
discussion after the worship service and result in interaction and

TABLE IV

Total Membership
Conversion growth - 131
Transfer growth - 95

Male   ◇

Female   ◇

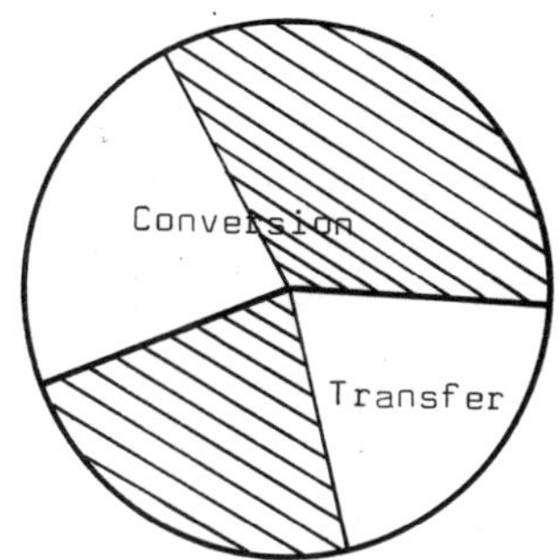

TABLE V

Analysis of membership

A - Regular attendance - 141
B - Absent for Study - 23
C - Married out - 17
D - Abroad - 29
E - Moved - 16

Male   ◇

Female   ◇

TABLE VI
REGULAR ATTENDANCE

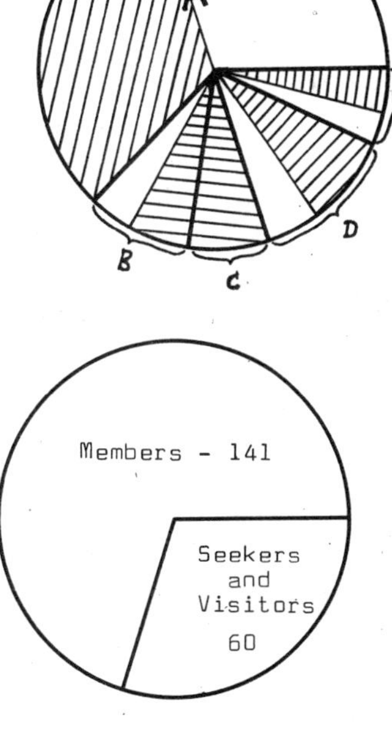

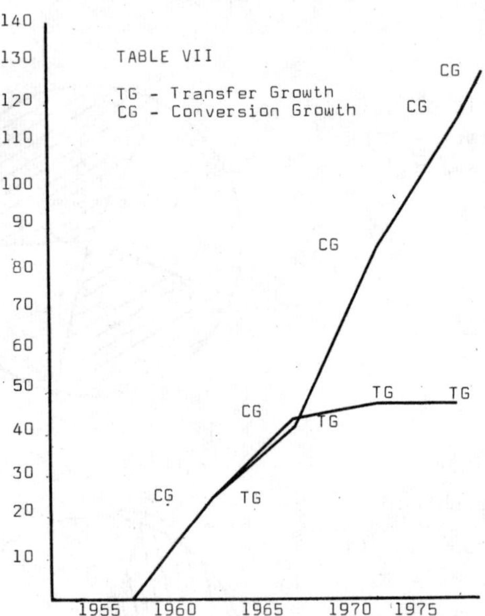

confrontation with challenges and opportunities for evangelism.

2. Lay people inviting and introducing seekers. The young people are most effective in introducing other young people. Women are also noted for regularly inviting and bringing seekers to the worship services. Businessmen and men in the older age bracket tend to speak to their own social and age group. In other words, members discern needs and receptivity of their friends, relatives, and neighbors and feel confident in inviting them to the church.

3. The pastor and his wife. Rev. Lin is a graduate of the Taiwan Theological Seminary. Until he came to Tok-heng a year ago, he was in industrial evangelism serving a large factory in the Kaoshiung area. He has a deep concern for evangelism and a deep empathy for the spiritual and social needs of the people. Pastor Lin has an honest, open and <u>biblical</u> approach to individual needs and church problems. He is a dynamic speaker and has the charisma which is infectious and challenging. He handles matters in an efficient and urgent manner. He is humble, open to ideas and welcomes cooperation. He is musically gifted as well. His desire to serve the Lord and His church

the humble, Spirit-led way he does it makes him a much-in-demand
speaker and a committee member with the larger churches as well. This
may tend somewhat to distract him from the "sheepfold" and the "sheep
not yet of the fold." While he feels that he relates well to older
people, he feels the need to work in the special ministry of relating
to young people.

Mrs. Lin graduated from the Tainan Theological Seminary with a
degree in kindergarten work. The church plans to provide a church
kindergarten in the new building. She supports her husband in the
church program, leads the women's meetings and assists him in the visitation work of the church. Mrs. Lin has a special gift for counseling with women who are facing family problems. Church members
bring her in contact with women who need help of this kind. Through
her counseling and evangelistic concern she has been able to lead
many of these women to the Lord. She impresses one as a keen listener
and compassionate observer. She is a person of a deep spiritual concern
and has an efficient and pragmatic approach to the situation before her.

Lay people readily express their opinion that the pastor and his
wife are the key to the progress of the church. Rev. and Mrs. Lin
carefully give constant recognition and glory to the Lord for any expression concerning the work or appreciation for their ministry.

4. Student activities. The Tuesday evening meeting of the Christian students form a chapter of the Christian Student Fellowship off
campus. The fellowship ministers to the well-known boys' school opposite the church. It is another opening to care for Christian young
men and to help then to lead their friends to the Lord. During important
sports events in the nearby stadium on Sunday mornings, the young people of the church are organized to hand out tracts to people. They
leave for the stadium shortly after the morning worship service.

CHURCH GROWTH PRINCIPLES AT WORK IN TOK-HENG CHURCH

1. A homogeneous church community. The socio-economic make-up
of the church is a strong homogeneous middle class of Taiwanese-speaking and predominantly middle-age businessmen. This makes for a solid
home base where no effort is needed to foster understanding, etc. Within the church we also find development along homogeneous lines of age,
sex, and social status. This has a definite relationship to growth
patterns.

2. Web movements. These are along the lines of family relationships through which a number of complete families have been brought
into the church.

3. Involvement of laity. The members of this church are aware
of their privilege and responsibility to be witnesses for the Lord.
They are the church's contact with the world and with those who are
receptive in it. The church has an open door, a listening ear and a
relevant message for their seeking friends. The objective of the pastor is to help each member to be a more conscious and efficient soul-
winner through an education program.

4. The concept of church growth goes beyond their own congregation as is evidenced by the scattering of the members to help in
planting new churches in areas where these members live. Growth of
the Tok-heng church has not been phenomenal but it has been steady
and strong. The reservoir of seekers and of potential seekers is well
filled and the channels for feeding it are many. This reservoir is
a challenging growth potential. The immediate community of people
relating to the Christians is five times the actual membership of the
church.

5. Nurture and guidance of Christians in their Christian pilgrim-
age is strong and responsibly administered. The careful procedure
in transferring members into and out of the church is one evidence
of this.

Each person brought to a personal encounter and relationship to
our Lord and Savior, Jesus Christ, has a unique experience and testimony. Many say, "It is a mystery," and "The Lord brought it about."
At the same time it is fascinating to observe all the facets of the
church life and the interacting of people which contribute to the successful work of the Holy Spirit in maintaining the number of seekers.
One readily observes that the Tok-heng church is a church with a
"people-to-people" program.

The involvement of members in the total ministry of the church
emphasizes the importance and role of each member. It builds loyalty
to the Lord and His church and is a challenge to other members to let
his/her light shine more brightly. "As every man hath received the
gift, even so minister the same one to another, as good stewards of
the manifold grace of God. If any man speaks, let him speak as the
oracles of God; if any man ministers, let him do it as of the ability

which God giveth: that God may be glorified through Jesus Christ,
to whom be praise and dominion for ever and ever. Amen." I Peter 10:11.

The membership of the church is an important factor in providing
a fine support structure for even greater church growth.

CONCLUSION

In my study of the church there have been many observations which
are very inspiring and commendable. These are a few suggestions which
could be considered in the future:

1. The proposed training for "every believer a soul winner" should
incorporate training in evaluation and utilization of bridges and resources for more effective use of the opportunities in the church and
the community for evangelism. The use of graphs and records could
become useful tools in evaluation.

2. Projects such as the proposed kindergarten and the continuing
student program for the nearby Boys' Middle School should receive careful evaluation, taking into consideration the overall investment of
funds, buildings, personnel, and the time needed to run these programs.
The overall objectives in operating these programs should be clearly
in mind and could be checked against the experiences of other churches
which have the same types of programs. Are the stated objectives realistic? Will they drain interest and resources from the priorities of
evangelism and church growth in the Tok-heng area and other outreach
areas? Are they an entry into homes and lives for evangelism?

The Tok-heng church speaks the language of the people in more
than one way. It relates to a homogenous society and involves the
largest possible number of believers in the work and witness of the
fellowship. The church seems to convey a vitally important Gospel
message with warmth, urgency, and relevance to the spiritually hungry.
We have noted that church growth principles are spontaneously applied
while at the same time plans are carefully laid for further training
of members for a greater harvest in the home meetings, joint Gospel
center and church outreaches in nearby areas. Thus greater growth
can be envisioned.

Finally, I feel led to believe that the Tok-heng church is a
very precious work of the Lord and very dear to Him. Blessed are its
members and all who seek Him there in spirit and in truth. The church
provides hope for those people in the area who look longingly to Zion

for the Salvation of the Lord. The Lord's saying in Isaiah 62:3 is applicable to the Tok-heng church: "Thou shalt also be a crown of glory in the hand of the Lord and a diadem in the hand of thy God."

ABOUT THE AUTHOR

Rev. J.N. Vandenberg is a missionary of the General Conference Mennonite Church, Commission on Overseas Mission, headquarters in Newton, Kansas. He was appointed to Taiwan upon invitation of "The Fellowship of Mennonite Churches in Taiwan" and assigned by the same to a partnership ministry of evangelism, church planting and pastor-at-large. Vandenberg began serving in Taiwan in 1956.

Chapter 5

THE CHILUNG CHURCH
A CHURCH GROWTH STUDY

The Chilung Church is a good example of a dynamic Mainlander church which has encountered a rapidly changing society, and today finds itself in a predominantly Taiwanese society in which most receptive Mainlanders have already been reached. The church thus stands at the crossroads and must come up with some workable solutions to hard problems if it is to continue to see dynamic growth and influence in the future.

We offer this study as a useful example, hopeful that it will speak to many churches in a similar situation. It is our prayer that the following report will prove both instructive and helpful.

Our basic approach to the study of this church has been one of personal interview. These sessions included Pastor and Mrs. Shao, individual lay people such as youth group leaders as well as a non-Christian wife in the neighborhood. Questions were directed primarily to matters pertaining to the dynamics of leadership, training, lay involvement, evangelism, the place of prayer, scripture, group dynamics, etc. Notes were made during interviews and the subsequent write-up reviewed by church leaders before final preparation for publication.

By way of personal note, I must at the outset of this report express my deep respect and appreciation for Pastor and Mrs. Shao-hsu In fairness to them it should be pointed out that they were unaware that the Church Growth Society had chosen their church for comparative study purposes. Despite the lack of adequate forewarning the Shaos, together with other church leaders, cooperated in every way, demonstrating not only their willingness to share their church life with an outsider, but also to provide food and lodging, plus many hours of patient interview time during my several visits. Besides the

opportunity for interview, I also enjoyed the chance to sit in on
a number of meetings and was even invited to share in the young people's meeting and the Sunday morning services. From this I'm sure
the reader will agree that the Chilung church presents a friendly
open heart towards outsiders, no small virtue in today's cold and impersonal city life.

GENERAL DESCRIPTION

A. Social Setting

    The Chilung church is located at #11 Yen Ping Street in the
southern downtown section of Chilung, also known as the Ren-Ai District.

Chilung Church

Daughter Church

    The building, a well-marked square reinforced concrete structure,
is built for economy of space and usefulness. Its location on the
hillside provides a commanding view of the immediate neighborhood.
    The daughter church is located ten minutes away by taxi on Tung
Hsin-ly, Alley 3, No. 34.

The neighborhood surrounding the mother church is middle to upper-class, predominantly Taiwanese-speaking with a sprinkling of Mainlanders. The area is largely residential along the side of the hill,
but entirely commercial along the mainstreet, Ren Er Lu, below. Scattered throughout the area are other families whose heads work in government offices mostly relating to the Chilung Harbor with its extensive shipping business, marine and customs offices. Others are involved in teaching and still others in civil offices of the Chilung
city. Poverty is not a part of this area.

There is a high degree of social mobility in the Chilung church
environs. This is partly due to the uncertain living patterns of
those who work on board ships as well as the fluctuations in employ-
ment conditions common to most port cities where commerce is tied to
world markets. This, together with a drifting of youth into the capital city of Taipei in search of better jobs and education, especially
among Mainland families less rooted in the Chilung area, makes for a
highly fluid population and a rapid turn over of membership in Mandarin-
speaking churches.

One other point of important note, the Chilung church is surrounded by eight other churches all within a distance of one kilometer.

B. History and Growth

The following historical sketch is a free translation of excerpts
from an anniversary brochure commemorating the 26th year of the Chilung church.

1. Period of Beginnings (June 1946-December 1950). From 1946,
Chinese from the Mainland have continued to settle in Chilung taking
up livelihoods in commerce, civil service and education. Due to
linguistic problems many Christians have had to travel to Mandarin-
speaking churches in Taipei for Sunday worship. Most, however, remained in Chilung with no place to worship. In 1947 a brother, Chin,
was able to appropriate the use of the assembly hall in the Customs
Building which was used for a short time. From here the group later
changed to Presbyterian facilities for afternoon meetings up through
1950. Subsequently, a Norwegian missionary opened a preaching hall
on Yi-Er Road which the Mandarin group began attending on Sunday mornings. Upon the departure of the missionary the work was left in the
hands of the Mainland Christians who continued through July 1953, at
which time they moved to their new church building on the present Yen

Ping Road location.

2.   Period of Hardships (January 1951-March 1953). From the
beginning in 1947 through 1951, numbers of Mainlanders attending the
early Chilung church group continued to grow. However, the early
fifties witnessed the arrival of other denominations including the
Baptists and Lutherans, all of which established new works in the
Chilung area. The results were predictable. Many who earlier worshipped with the independent group now began leaving for the denominations of their earlier affiliation on the Mainland. This sudden
loss of numbers was nearly disastrous for the original group which
continued on, greatly depleted and no longer large enough to require
more than a small classroom for worship. Subsequently, one of the
three leaders was temporarily disabled following an accident. At
this point voices were raised in favor of disolving the group. Those
desiring to press on won the day, however, and spirits rose once
again to the challenge to move ahead and trust God.

3.   Church Building Period (February-June 1953). During this
period, after much searching and prayer, the present site (94 ping)
on Yen Ping Road was found and rented though not purchased for 20
years. Despite escalating costs of building and lack of monies the
Lord graciously provided through the generous gifts of His people and
building began. At first a bamboo structure, then a more permanent
concrete and steel structure provided adequate facilities for the
growing congregation. At the time of ground breaking, May 10,
the believers numbered just over thirty. The new building was dedicated on August 23, 1953 and Elder Wu Yung addressed the group on
"The Church and The Holy Spirit." This was followed by a number of
evangelistic and deeper-life meetings and finally the calling of a
full time pastor, brother Shao Hsu, February 1954.

4.   Period of Expansion (November 1954-February 1969). Seven
additions to the original building were made between 1954 and 1969
when the present complex was completed. Together with the cost of
building the sister church on Tung hsin Road in 1969, God's people
raised a total of over two million N.T. dollars or well over $50,000.00
U.S. currency, no small amount at that time.

While statistics covering annual baptisms, attendance and membership are scanty, it is obvious that the life of the church has been
marked by periods of remarkable growth from the first 30 or so believers

74

in 1953 to an average attendance of about 120 (total for both churches) today.

It is altojether clear what patterns of growth have been most marked over the years. Doubtless many members have come as individuals, reached during the evangelistic meetings especially in the earlier years. It would seem, however, with the gradual decrease of receptive individual Mainlanders that an increasing number of local Taiwanese have been reached through the day-to-day witness of the Chilung church believers. A few of these have been heads of homes and some of these have in turn reached their own children and relatives. To date Pastor Shao reckons a total of 47 full or partial families for the mother and daughter churches. Following are a couple of illustrations of how whole families have come to Christ:

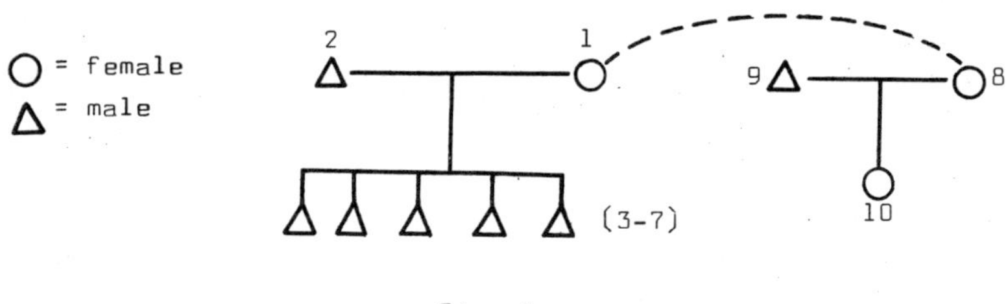

Fig. 1

Number one is Mrs. Wu, won to Christ by the witness and friendship of Chilung church believers. She in turn led her husband, five sons, friend (no. 8), her husband and their daughter to Christ. Evidently the church had a part in influencing Mrs. Wu's children, but the deciding factor was her own enthusiastic sharing of Christ which was done largely along kinship and friendship lines. This all took about ten years.

In Figure 2 we have a grandmother, Mrs. Chang, (#1) leading her daughter-in-law (#2) to Christ, subsequently followed by three granddaughters and two grandsons (#3-7) into the faith and finally her son #8). Again a whole family has turned to Christ largely through one person's witness and influence. In this case the total process took about 20 years.

Meanwhile an increasing number of young people are coming

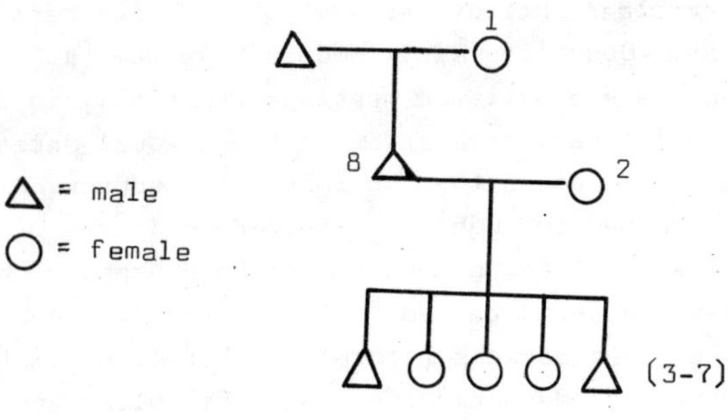

Fig. 2

to Christ at the Chilung church, but family conversions are not resulting in many cases especially among the Taiwanese. This seems largely
due to the resistance of traditional folk religion and associated beliefs, but may also indicate the possibility that a Mainlander church
does not easily attract older Taiwanese-speaking Chinese.

One final note should be added to clarify the relationship of
the Chilung church to other churches on the island. From its beginning, the Chilung church has been independent. Although there were
several early stages when the Chilung church believers worshipped together with other groups, it has maintained an independent status
throughout its history. There is a loose-knit arrangement for fellowship, pulpit sharing, and cooperation in summer youth camps among a
number of other Mandarin-speaking churches.

5. Present Structure. A cross section of the Chilung church
today would reveal a primarily Mainlander oriented church with an increasing core of Taiwanese young people. In terms of occupational
background the membership would look roughly as follows, based on a
total of about 140 middle to upper-class people:

(This breakdown was a rough estimate provided by the church leaders.) One is impressed at once with the large numbers from Marine
(those working with shipping companies, many serving on ships), student and teacher categories, the three most mobile of the larger occupational groups in Chilung. Of the present membership of 140

76

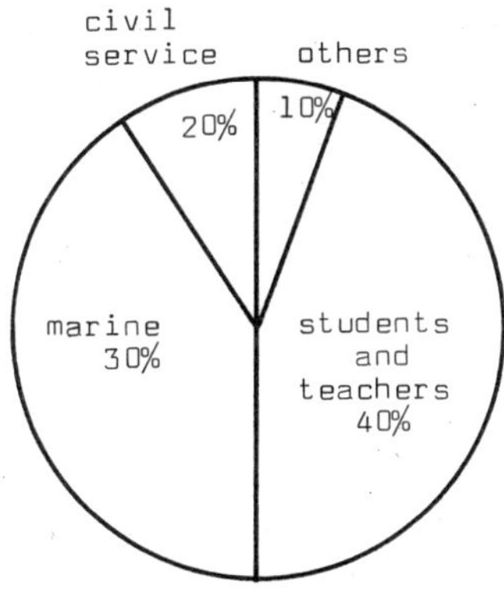

believers, most are from Che-chiang and Chiang-su provinces. Since
1951 a total of 506 have been baptized. 203 of these were from Che-
chiang, 74 Chiang-su, 47 were Taiwanese, 43 from Shan Tung, 29 from
Fu Chien, 20 from Sz Chuan, 90 from other places. This points up another important fact. In terms of cultural and linguistic background
the Chilung church is a mosaic of homogeneous units (the largest of
which is from the province of Che-chiang) and is surrounded largely
by a neighborhood of Taiwanese. An anomalous situation to say the
least.

A word concerning the organizational structure of the Chilung
church will help us to follow the lines of authority within the congregation. Basically the structure appears as follows:

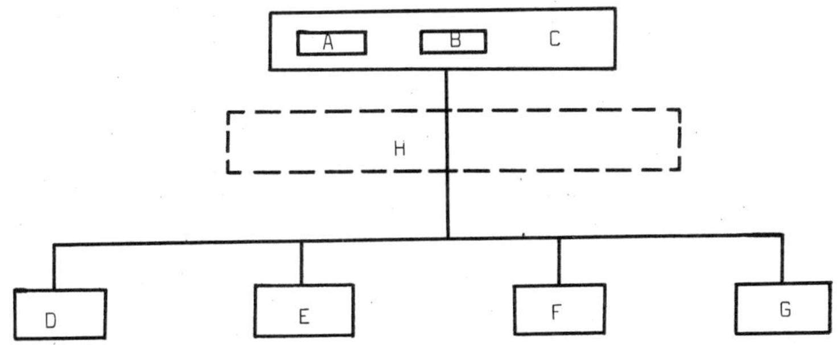

A - Juridical body

B - Board of trustees

C - Tung Kung Huei (co-worker's group)

D - Small groups for executing the nine ministries of the church

    1. Prayer
    2. Evangelism
    3. Visitation
    4. Literature
    5. Education
    6. Ordinances (baptism, communion, etc.)
    7. Reception (receiving guests, ushering, etc.)
    8. Business
    9. Finances

E - Women's work

F - Men's work

G - Youth work

H - Annual Members' Meeting

It should be noted that the above diagram is an approximation of the ways in which the lines of ministry fall. No such chart has been drawn so this was the first attempt to visualize the organizational structure.

Boxes "A" and "B" represent the churches legal body for holding property and administrating legal matters according to government requirements. These are both composed of the same three leaders who in turn are part of the seven making up the Co-workers Committee. The latter appears to be the highest authority for the general run of the church life and activities. All groups are answerable to this group whose main representatives are the pastor and his wife. Even the Annual Members' Meeting which meets once a year must submit to the authority of the Co-worker's Committee.

The large number of "small groups" under "D" are led largely by male leaders. In other areas of the church, however, most of the church workers are women and a large number of those are quite young.

New members of the Co-worker's Committee (also called deacons) are chosen by the existing leadership structure on the basis of experience and gifts for ministry which they have demonstrated. Leadership at all levels is chosen on this same principle. The role of the Holy Spirit plus the individual's desire to serve are key elements in the process of discovering leaders. This is an interesting con= trast to the annual meeting held by many churches in which leaders are formally elected.

EQUIPPING THE SAINTS

In this section we will look at those areas of ministry directed at the building up of believers. In order to appreciate the kind and quality of ministries we must first look at a profile of the two main leaders, Pastor and Mrs. Shao.

A. Profile of Leadership

Pastor Shao-hsu was born and reared in Tien Ching, mainland China. Eldest of three children in a non-Christian family, he was converted in a church called the Chung-Hua Chitu Chiao-huei in 1945. As a young man Shao joined the navy and during the years of increasing Communist threat was stationed on a small island off Ching Tsu, Shan Tung, where he served as an accountant. It was here that he had his first opportunity to serve Christ. Subsequent to the fall of China, Shao was relocated at Chilung harbor where he soon met others of like faith.

Pastor Shao-hsu is quiet-mannered, soft-spoken, and gifted as both teacher and leader. In good Chinese tradition he leads largely through example. His teaching method is of special interest. Both in early morning prayers as well as in Sunday school, Pastor Shao teaches largely through well-placed questions, probing and searching the minds of those present until the answer, based upon the passage at hand, is forthcoming. The more common Chinese custom of lecturing seems to have little place in his pedagogy. Shao also has a fine grasp of Scripture content despite his lack of any seminary or formal theological training. I would sum up Pastor Shao's leadership as low profile, firm but gentle.

Mrs. Shao, born in Shan Tung, is a third-generation Christian. Following her graduation from the Southern Baptist Seminary she married Mr. Shao in 1959. Her influence in the church is very marked. Being a women of much energy and deep dedication she throws herself tirelessly into most areas of church work whether preaching on Sunday, teaching Sunday School, coaching the young people, leading Sunday afternoon evangelistic teams or teaching Bible Study groups. Mrs. Shao's temperament is firm but loving. Her authority is not questioned and young people look to her as friend and counselor. These two, called Uncle Shao and Teacher P'eng, have learned that art of leadership which allows maximum freedom for the development and exercise of gifts especially among the youth. They are also loved and respected by the adults whom they have served for over sixteen years.

Rather than describe the many meetings which are held on a
weekly and monthly basis we will examine distinctive emphases such
as prayer, Bible reading, small group dynamics and so on.

B. Prayer

A deep and persistant emphasis upon prayer is a distinctive mark
of the Chilung Church. On national holidays an average of 40 believers
gather from six to nine AM in small groups for prayer, Bible study
and sharing from current devotional reading. From 6-7 a.m. every
morning except Sunday, the Shao's plus a number of lay people, join
for Bible Study, praise and prayer. Prayer is both individual as well
as corporate and prayer items are specific. Prayer may be observed
in almost every meeting in the church. God's miraculour provision
for the costs of land and building is attributed to prayer. The Sunday outreach group always prays before going forth to witness. Believers are taught to make prayer a vital part of their personal de-
votions. On Wednesday evenings those attending prayer meeting sit in
a circle. The first 45 minutes are given to prayer during which time
all kneel together. Following is another 45 minutes of sharing that
which each has received from his or her reading of Daily Bread. Sometimes testimonies are also shared. A whole network of special weekly
prayer groups is organized every fall and terminates at the time of
the annual Christmas Evangelistic meetings towards which all prayer
has been directed.

C.   Scriptures

The Scriptures also play a very large role in the life of the
Chilung Church. Of particular interest is an all-church emphasis upon daily Bible reading using a Chinese version of Scripture Union useful for both adults as well as teenagers. The wide-spread use of this
material by church members evidently came after a number of years of
faithful exhortation and instruction in the importance of systematic
and regular Bible Study. The advantage of every member's daily reading the same passage is obvious. The passage in question on any given
day may become the subject of the pastor's sermon, the focus for the
weekly Bible study groups on Friday night, or the subject for mutual
sharing by the young people on Saturday evenings. An element of
accountability is added since one may be asked at any time to share
what he or she has gleaned from private Bible study that day.

The high profile of God's Word is also seen in the emphasis upon
Scripture memory, Scripture verses on walls, carrying of Bible, etc.
Believers often memorize small booklets of specially chosen Scriptures
such as "God's Answers."

D. Small Groups

The use of small groups is a distinct characteristic of the Chilung
Church. Over ten small groups meet each week varying from women's to
weekly Bible study groups. These small intimate groups allow not only
for a sense of closeness and individual concern, but opportunity also
arises for all to share in group leadership responsibilities. It is
most likely in these small groups that God s people not only discover
their own gifts for ministry but also come to recognize them in one
another. It is in the small groups where believers share with one another their questions or discoveries from daily Bible reading. The
small group is also used in home meetings for women as well as men.
On Sunday afternoons a number of young people, together with the pastor
or his wife, go out into a Chilung suburb for door-to-door lay evangelism. Here again the small group approach is used so that each member
of a group of three or four finds opportunity to witness, to give out
literature and to generally feel that he or she is having a definite
part in establishing a new "preaching point" which they hope will grow
into a church.

E. Evangelism

Evangelism is one of the major concerns of the Chilung Church.
Special evangelistic meetings were held often in the early years of
the church. The emphasis continues today with one special evangelistic sermon every first Sunday of the month. Pastor Shao indicates
that of 29 baptisms per year, which the church has been averaging the
past five years, most are the fruit of contacts made by lay Christians.
Evangelistic concern is to be found in the Sunday morning preaching
service (evening meetings are always for the Lord's Supper), jail and
hospital visitation and Sunday outreach. The pastor is busy during
summer months, speaking at youth conferences for various groups up and
down the island. In 1969 a daughter church was begun in a nearby area.
The daughter church has now its own outreach of visitation and special
meetings thus continuing the evangelistic emphasis of the mother church.
The young people of these two churches hold one evangelistic emphasis
series each semester. Speakers are chosen from their own church and

these meetings are specially designed to reach other youth. The youth
evangelistic program includes a 20 minute message, testimonies, music
and counseling.

CHRISTIAN LITERATURE

Christian literature is fairly well used by the Chilung Church.
Besides a small library of books available for all to read, they receive a dozen or so Christian periodicals, including a Chinese version
of _Decision Magazine_. The latter is subscribed for in large numbers.
Every believer is encouraged to order two personal copies plus extra
copies to sell to others. For each extra copy purchased, the church
pays one-third. These in turn are sold at one-third of cost to encourage reading by others. Copies of the weekly church bulletin including all weekly activities, special prayer needs from both churches,
are mailed out to those who are temporarily away in the army, at sea,
in other parts of the island or abroad. Fifty copies go out each week.
This proves to be an important link keeping those temporarily absent
from drifting and reminding them of the continuing concern of God's
people in Chilung. Many, too, send their offerings. Thus, though
they are far from home they are encouraged to keep in touch with God
and with their home church.

DIVERSIFIED APPROACH TO YOUTH

A diversified approach to youth is reflected in the number of separate young people's groups meeting each Saturday evening. These number three and include primary through middle school, high school through
college and those out in secular jobs in society. The separation of
the second and third groups above is very strategic since it reflects
a clear understanding of the distinct set of needs, experiences, and
problems which are entirely different for the two groups. On one hand,
college and high schoolers fellowship around those experiences largely
related to their academic pursuits and school life while those with
secular jobs share a totally different experience, reflecting their
daily exposure to a highly impersonal, competitive society of daily
work and business.

POTENTIAL PROBLEMS

No church is perfect and the Chilung church is no exception. It seems to have its own peculiar set of problems which we do well to consider.

A MAINLAND CHURCH SURROUNDED BY TAIWANESE

Perhaps the most serious problem arises from an accident of history: a Mainland church surrounded by a sea of Taiwanese. This would not be serious if the potential for continuing Mainland converts were still strong. It seems rather that the number of receptive Mainlanders still uncommitted to any church are few indeed. In other words, the potential source for traditional lines of growth is drying up. Converts must come increasingly from younger Mandarin-speaking Taiwanese.

One possible direction to explore is that of a Taiwanese worship service distinct from existing services. This would be entirely in Taiwanese and would be geared for the older generation unable to speak Mandarin. This, however, would require the gradual development of a church within a church which is never easy. However, the leadership of the church is aware of the problem and is open to whatever direction the Lord may give in the future as they consider increased evangelistic outreach among the Taiwanese.

SHORTAGE OF TRAINED LAY LEADERS

While the Sunday School and work among women seems to be well provided with maturing lay leadership, there is a notable absence of male adult leadership. Among the 30 to 50-age range, believers come and go with amazing frequency. Many potential male leaders are away at sea or have been called elsewhere by their professions. As a result the Chi Lung Church has hardly any active male members aged 30 to 50 from whom to train for badly needed leadership for the men's work.

PLANNING FOR ADVANCE

The Chi Lung Church has done much towards organizing itself for effective evangelism. Of special note is the emphasis upon individual responsibility to be a sharer of the Good News. Specific goals for reaching stated numbers of new believers have been carefully set. In order to further strengthen this program, the Chi Lung Church needs to set intermediate stages at which time progress may be evaluated and individual church members given opportunity to report. If original goals prove unrealistic then they may be adjusted upward or downward.

Follow Up for New Converts

Like many other churches in Taiwan, the Chi Lung Church is experiencing difficulty in devising effective plans for follow-up of new or potential converts. Some churches are finding it necessary to build intermediate stages whereby people newly-reached are first nurtured through a period of home Bible study and repeated visits before being brought into the actual church building for worship. "Project Philip" has proven helpful as a Bible study program adaptable to such needs in a number of churches.

Marriage

As the pressures of urbanization and industrialization erode the traditional family patterns, increasing numbers of young couples are experiencing marital difficulties. The problem of suitable matches for Christian young people continues to be a major problem facing pastors in large urban churches. Marriage counseling, which has come to play such an important role in western churches, is increasingly needed in Taiwan. Somehow the church must prove itself to be a place of help for young people trapped in various marital problems. Even those who have suffered through the trauma of divorce must find a place of healing and hope within the church family. Answers are not ready at hand. However, the awareness of the Chi Lung Church leadership to these needs is a hopeful sign for the future.

CONCLUSION

We close this study with a number of observations growing out of the above study. Most of these are in no way unique with the Chilung Church. One could safely say that they are representative of many other churches which find themselves in similar circumstances.

First, the Chilung Church will in the days ahead need to address itself to the problems of changing receptivity of the surrounding population, the need for developing strategy and leadership for reaching

Taiwanese, both Mandarin-speaking youth as well as Min-nan-speaking
adults. The church will thus need to prepare for the day when the
body of believers will be primarily of local Taiwanese, very possibly
still operating largely in Mandarin but reflecting increasingly the
cultural distinctives of Taiwan.

Second, with these possibilities in mind, a greater emphasis will
need to be given to reaching whole families for Christ. A strong
local-born and trained Taiwanese sheperd-evangelist will be a must for
this ministry. This man should be an understudy of Pastor Shao learning from him and working with him somewhat akin to the role of associate pastor in western churches.

Third, increased attention must be given in the future to social
problems which are eroding the family, especially problems of divorce
and separation, mis-matched marriages, working parents and so on. Many
of these are best handled within the church where people can experience
forgiveness from God, acceptance by God's family and involvement in
meaningful family worship and activities.

. Finally, the serious gap in the 30 to 50 age span of male believers must be wrestled with and some possible solutions worked out.
Ideally, future leadership should be developing from within this group.
Unless men of this age range can be reached in the near future, serious problems lie ahead. There is always the possibility of outsiders
moving in from other churches but this is not ideal for the Chi Lung
Church. Attractive programs for men need to be launched such as
presently attract a large number of women. This project should be
high on the priority list for the future.

Many open doors beckon the people of God in the Chilung Church
but many adversaries await each attempt to move forward. However,
viewed from the stance of openness to change and new patterns of ministry and the assurance that God wills that the lost be reached and
the devil defeated, the church is faced with a future of great potential for advance and expansion.

We are confident that the Chi Lung Church is open to God's direction. We are confident, moreover, that as God's people wait upon Him
in prayer, He will direct into the unknown paths of the future. As
the Word of God is faithfully taught and lived, He will raise up new
leaders to help in the great task ahead. As the congregation continues
its great tradition of prayer, and evangelism, people who once seemed

like hardy, stony ground will in time become aware of their great need
and begin to seek the Lord.

     May the same faithful prayer-answering God who worked miracles in
the past lead and bless this congregation in the years ahead. May
they indeed live as a spiritual lighthouse in this sin-filled port city
where so many now live without Christ and without hope.

ABOUT THE AUTHOR

     Alan Frederick Gates was born in Calgary, Alberta, Canada on
May 6, 1931. He received his Bachelor of Arts degree in Geology from
the University of British Columbia in Vancouver in 1954. In 1959, he
obtained his Bachelor of Divinity degree from Fuller Theological Seminary in Pasadena, California. He and his wife, Sharon, proceeded to
the island of Taiwan where he served as a missionary from 1959 to
1964. While on furlough in the United States, Gates received his Master of Arts degree from the School of World Mission at Fuller Theological Seminary in 1966. He returned to Taiwan under the Conservative
Baptist Foreign Mission Society. In 1971, Gates again enrolled at the
School of World Mission at Fuller Theological Seminary and earned the
Doctor of Missiology degree prior to returning to the field. He is
currently serving in a teaching and church development ministry in
Taiwan.

Chapter 6

1964 Photo of Pastor Hsieh & Family

FREEDOM ROAD BAPTIST CHURCH
A Church Unafraid of Challenges

Freedom Road Baptist Church is a large, two-story building located on a major street just blocks from the heart of Taichung. The sanctuary is on the second floor. The classrooms are underneath. A second building to the right houses a bookstore, correspondence office, girls' dormitory and pastor's office. The building is larger than most churches in Taiwan. Its people have a vision that is larger than many other Christians. As you ascend the broad staircase to the sanctuary, you are reminded of the words of Isaiah 2:3, ".. and many people shall come and say ...'Come, let us go up to the ... house of the God of Jacob; that He may teach us His ways'." Many people have ascended these stairs and found the Lord within. Many more have been solidly taught His ways there. From its beginning in 1952 through the end of 1976, 1448 have entered the waters of the believer's baptism. Another 301 have transferred in for a total of 1749 new members in 24 years.

During this same time, Freedom Road Baptist Church has sent an amazing number of men and women into full-time Christian service.

From this congregation have come 36 Christian workers, about one-half of them are pastors. Another 17 workers have come out of the chapels and churches planted by this mother church. Another 11 have entered full-time service after leaving this church and joining another. Directly or indirectly, 64 full-time Christian workers stand as noble testimony to the spiritual vigor and strength of one dedicated shepherd and his congregation of believers.

Freedom Road Baptist Church was established on Mother's Day, 1952. It dedicated its present building on Mother's Day, 1955. It has lived up to the symbolism of these dates. Today it has already become a spiritual grandmother. In 19 years it has given birth to ten additional churches in Taichung city or county, has assisted in the founding of three more and has observed two of its daughter churches give birth to two more churches. A total of 15 churches thus look to Freedom Road Church as their spiritual mother.

Church growth is not as easy as it was 20 years ago. But this never becomes an excuse to rest upon past accomplishments. After a three year baptismal slump from 1971-1973, Freedom Road Church caught a new vision for church growth. The result? In 1975 it baptized over twice as many as three years earlier. (See Figure #1) Obviously this church deserves a closer look. It is indeed a large, solid church but the story lies with its people and its leader, not in its building.

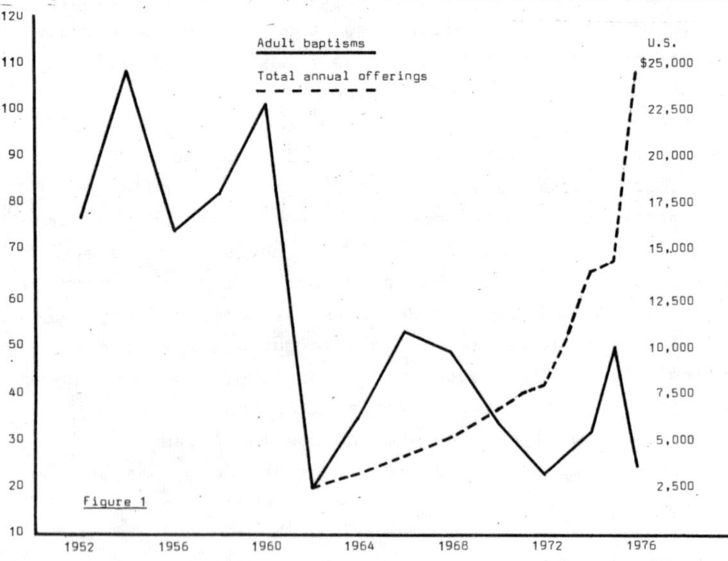

88

HISTORICAL DEVELOPMENT

The many accomplishments of Freedom Road Baptist Church did not
"just happen." God used a number of factors. One primary growth
factor arose out of a combination of historical events. Church growth
studies have repeatedly shown that sociological or political upheaval
opens wide the door to change. Confused or uprooted people require
new answers. Their former foundations are broken; their aspirations
crushed. The old is stripped away. What they choose to replace the
old or what values they now adopt depends largely upon the availability
of meaningful, integrated solutions. The deeper the plow of adversity
cuts, the greater the demand for new solutions. But freshly plowed
soil does not lie fallow for long. To produce a harvest, the seed must
be planted quickly, in sufficient quantities. The harvest will belong
to those who arrive first with the best seed.

During the 1950's the mainlander community in Taiwan was just
such an uprooted, refugee community. Never had upheaval so opened so
many hearts to the Gospel. Never in the history of China missions did
a greater percentage of people become Christian in less time.[1] From
1948-1950 well over one million crushed, disillusioned refugees poured
into Taiwan from the fallen China mainland. Gone was everything they
held dear to them; they had been defeated. During the decade to follow
ten's of thousands accepted Christianity as their new foundation for
life. But by the late 1950's this surge of converts had almost ceased.
The largest "mainlander" churches in Taiwan today are those established
earliest in the 1950's.

Freedom Road Baptist Church was one of the earliest mainlander
churches in Taichung. In November, 1951, a colorful veteran American
missionary, Miss Addie Cox chose Taichung as the site for her work.
Her philosophy had always been clear and simple. Go where the need is,
where the soil is receptive, start a new work and move on as soon as a
replacement can be found. Having already planted one church in Keelung,
she started her second project in Taichung. Work began in a rented,
wood-frame structure near the Taichung Railway Station. Through
preaching, visitation, tract distribution plus a good deal of courage
and perseverance, Miss Cox saw her new ministry flourish. In July,
1952, less than 10 months later, she turned over her new infant church
and headed back north to plant church number three in Taoyuan. Re-
placing her was the Rev. Chang Rung-chiang who remained only four months
for in the fall of 1952 the Baptist Seminary opened in Taipei and his

services were needed as the new dean of students.

During the following three years the church was successively served by three different missionary pastors and a Chinese woman evangelist. Exciting days of rapid growth followed. Evangelistic meetings of all types were held. Tract distribution, visitation, plus a vision for church planting all motivated these pioneer missionaries. Figure one reveals the tremendous conversion rate during this three year period. Such rapid growth required relocation into a larger building. The Mission purchased a choice piece of property only blocks from the heart of town yet a safe three blocks away from the noise and confusion of downtown commercial activity. It was a wise selection and one that would serve well as the hub of much outward expansion.

Not only did the church grow numerically during these days, it also began early to plant new churches. The mainlander community was a highly mobile group in the early 1950's. Where the Christians went they took their faith with them. In their first three years, Freedom Road Church planted four more churches. The first church in Changhua began through outdoor evangelistic meetings. In the following 20 months three more churches were planted. In each case the home of former members was used as the initial base for outreach. From each home grew a new church. Home churches was the method used for most of the other churches planted in the following two decades.

In 1955 the individual most responsible for shaping the future of this church arrived. Rev. Hsieh, Po-wu was led to the Lord under the ministry of the Salvation Army in Shantung province, north China. His earliest theological training was in the Salvation Army School in Peiping. After graduation he was sent back to Shantung for ministry. While there he was deeply influenced by the spiritual revival sweeping the entire province of Shantung during the 1930's.

Mr. Hsieh had a great burden for evangelism. Unable to support himself in full-time preaching during the chaotic days of World War II, Mr. Hsieh taught school instead. Whenever possible he would use his evenings for preaching in various home meetings. When the Salvation Army left his area, he joined the fast-growing, independent Assembly Hall church founded by Watchman Nee. From them he learned much about evangelism and lay mobilization.

In 1949 Mr. Hsieh came to Taiwan and taught in a girl's middle school. He also worked with the Assembly Hall brethren on weekends

and vacations but in 1953 he left them over doctrinal differences.
However, he continued his dual ministry of teaching and preaching until
March, 1955 when he became a full-time evangelist at the Freedom Road
Church.

Sensing his lack of theological training, he spent the next three
years commuting 110 miles north to Taipei where he attended the Southern Baptist Theological Seminary. In June, 1958 he graduated, was ordained and became the second Chinese pastor to serve this Taichung
church. From the following year, all missionaries associated with the
church served in an advisory capacity only. The church was now firmly
in the hands of mature Chinese leadership.

The rapid early growth of this church can be traced to a number
of factors, some already mentioned. First was the advantage of being
one of the earliest arrivals in the harvest field. Second was the
decision to early engage in both aggressive evangelism and strong
church planting ministries. Five new chapels planted and another
assisted during the first five years stand as testimony to their
vision of outreach. The church did not just content itself with
gathering members within its own four walls. "Giving yourself away"
to grow was a solid Biblical principle employed in planting new churches.
Third was the wise location. Only one other Mandarin-speaking church
is as strategically located near the heart of Taichung. It is a central-
city church. Fourth was the mission decision to grant complete autonomy
to this rapidly growing congregation at an early date. Continued mission-
support may have been counter-productive. In 1962 it became one of the
first Baptist churches to terminate all mission aid. In the congregation's own words "this decision enabled the brothers and sisters to
realize their own personal responsibility before God and to know that
to preach the Gospel, one must not be dependent on foreign resources.
We must rather depend upon and look to the founder of our faith -
Jesus Christ."[2]

As members continued to move on to other parts of Taichung and
beyond, they formed the nucleus for more new churches. A total of ten
churches was planted, seven of them during their first ten years. In
each case the initiative originated with the church, not the mission.
Money was in short supply in the Mandarin community during those days
and the cost for land and building was beyond the ability of the
average congregation. If a new chapel showed signs of real promise,
and if it could repay one-third of the total cost of land and property

within ten years, then the Southern Baptist Mission would underwrite
the original cost of land and building. This policy seemed to work
well at that point of Taiwan church history.

Freedom Road Baptist Church continues to minister primarily to
the mainlander - or Mandarin-speaking - community. About 85% of its
members are from this group of former refugees. They share much in
common. About one-third of the members are government employees. Another third are military personnel, teachers - again under government
employ - or students. The balance are housewives. Unlike many Taiwanese
churches which can draw from the business community, Freedom Road Church
has no wealthy and few professional-class members.[3] But as figure one indicates, this has not hampered their ability to give. During the 1973-
1975 recession when prices were spiraling and giving was decreasing,
Freedom Road Christians almost doubled their contributions. At the
end of 1976 with a total baptized membership of 591 - average Sunday
attendance was about 300 - they gave a total of US$25,800 or an average
of $43 per baptized member in a country where the average family earns
less than $300 per month.

A CHURCH IN ACTION

If you join the 10:00 a.m. Sunday morning worship at Freedom Road
Church you will be struck by a number of facts. One is the average of
300 worshippers which fill every section of the auditorium, about three
to four times as many as the average Mandarin church in Taichung. Lay
leaders conduct the service apart from the message, prayer and benedic-
tion given by the pastor. The Sunday bulletin provides a clue to the
number of weekly activities. Sunday morning is time for Sunday School
for 11 classes from kindergarten through adults. A missionary also
teaches an English Bible class. Monday is prison evangelism and a home
worship is held in the evening. Wednesday evening is Bible study and
prayer time. Friday the Women's Missionary Guild and Men's Fellowship
meet. On Saturday the choir practices and three different youth groups
gather. And on Saturday and Sunday afternoons for one month out of
every four, an average of 30-35 committed Christians fan out over the
city in door-to-door evangelism which is the current key to their growth.
Monday through Saturday mornings at 7:30 also find a nucleus of Christians gathered at the church for Bible study and prayer.

Growing churches are always marked by three special characteristics:

strong leadership, a burden for evangelism and an ability to utilize
the laity as unpaid co-workers. Freedom Road Church possesses all
three qualities.

Rev. Hsieh early displayed strong leadership potential, administrative competence and a real burden for evangelism. From his early
years as pastor, the church received a strong teaching ministry that
emphasized the need for a personal salvation, evangelistic outreach and
lay participation. In Pastor Hsieh's own words, the first two reasons
for the growth of this church are the unity of the congregation as ex-
pressed through their support of his leadership and their strong emphasis
on evangelistic outreach.

Leadership played a strong role in the formation of these attitudes.
In the mid-1960's, after an island-wide slump in new baptisms, the
Taiwan Baptist Convention, in cooperation with their other Asian sister
churches, voted to initiate a five year island-wide united evangelistic
outreach. (Known as the Yajou Jinsyin hwei Lyanhe budau yundung). Rev.
Hsieh was selected as the director for this program. For five years
all the churches used every means available to spread the Gospel.
Evangelistic rallies, choral groups from home and abroad, special lec-
tures on the college campuses in science and related areas were all
held. Even moon-astronaut, James Irwin, made special appearances in
schools and churches throughout Taiwan.

Pastor Hsieh firmly believes that a church will grow only when
the membership is totally involved in some form of evangelistic program.
Figure one confirms this thesis. During the relatively more receptive
era from 1961-1965 adult baptisms totaled 183. During the next five
years, the period of this evangelistic campaign, Freedom Road Church
added 30% more baptisms than in the previous five year period.

Even this experience did not satisfy Pastor Hsieh. He knew that
during the 1949-1959 era, mass evangelism was a quick, effective
method for church growth. During the next decade one had to work
much harder for fewer results. By 1969 with a stabilized society and
no more fear of insecurity, the appeal of mass evangelism had all but
disappeared. Although Campus Crusade had been invited in on several
occasions to train the laity for outreach, little happened. The non-
Christians were still not coming and the laity were not sufficiently
involved. The attraction of television introduced in 1968 and other
factors also combined to seriously reduce the number of new baptisms.[4]

"COMMUNITY EVANGELISM"_Key to New Church Growth

Pastor Hsieh needed a new vision - and he found it at the "Explo-74" evangelism training conference held in Seoul, Korea and attended by over 300,000 Asian delegates in August, 1974. The key was simple enough: if the people will not come to your church, then you, the church, must go to them! But how to do this? Clear goals, planning and training were needed. A new program which the church called "Community Evangelism" was born in Pastor Hsieh's mind. As a good administrator, he began by first sharing his vision with the church leaders. After they understood and approved it was shared with the total congregation. In October, 1974 just months after the Seoul conference, the program was started.

Pastor Hsieh began by pulpit teaching to prepare his people for a new evangelistic outreach, one that would be long lasting and far reaching. No one was pushed or compelled. "Community Evangelism" was placed in the perspective in which it belonged - to participate was a privilege. Registration for the training course was required and about 50 attended with 40 actual registrants.[5] The goal was a big one, the kind designed to inspire - every home in Taichung was to be reached with the Gospel! Taichung is a city of 600,000. Others would be needed to fulfill this goal. At the same time that his own church was being prepared for this new program, Pastor Hsieh was busy convincing other area churches of the desirability of their participation. He encouraged three other Baptist churches and seven non-Baptist churches to also become involved. He personally trained most of their leaders during the initial stage of the program.

The dynamics of this new program can be itemized as follows: Planning: To reach every home in Taichung, the city must be carefully surveyed and charted. First the city was divided into districts. Beginning with the area closest to the church, each district was further sub-divided into units according to streets or other geographical landmarks. Each block of homes was then given a number and assigned to a visitation team. Training: Since "Explo-74" was sponsored by Campus Crusade, Pastor Hsieh invited their local representatives to come to the church for the initial training program. After the initial four nights of training, all members were divided into three-man teams consisting of a man, a woman and a youth. For the following five nights they went out on an organized house-to-house visitation program. The results were encouraging. More important, the members were excited.

Unlike former evangelism training programs, this one required that they
absolutely follow through with actual visitation. Thereafter visitation
was conducted every Saturday and Sunday afternoon from 3-5 p.m. Action:
Going and doing what they had been taught was the essential key to the
program. Blessing comes from "doing" and not just "hearing" as Jesus
reminds us.[6] Freedom Road Church members were learning by "doing" the
will of Christ and not just "hearing" about it. But in early 1975 it
was evident that even the most zealous of Christians readily wearies
from a regular weekend program of evangelism. The program was revised.
Henceforth one month of every three would be reserved for intensive
evangelistic outreach. Now, on the first Friday night of the month,
Pastor Hsieh leads a two hour training and review session. The following
four weekends are set aside for visitation. At the end of the month,
all members take a well-deserved two month rest. Rather than to quickly
burn themselves out the revised system enables them to continue the program indefinitely. Prayer Chain: If "Community Evangelism" succeeds, it
is not just due to "techniques." All such programs readily flounder unless undergirded by prayer. Before each month of outreach, the whole
church is called to prayer. The Prayer Committee issues a prayer cal-
endar divided into 24 one hour periods. Members sign up for one hour
each. A non-stop 24 hours of prayer thereby provides the underpinning
for each new outward thrust. Prayer chains are used before many special
programs and always before any evangelistic meetings. Teamwork: Trained
by the Pastor, undergirded by prayer and well supplied with visitation
materials, the teams spread out to their assigned areas. If a man answers the door, the male member of the team takes the initiative. If a
woman greets them, the equivalent team member leads the conversation.
Should a youth first open the door, the youthful member of the team re-
ciprocates. One card is filled out for every contact made indicating
reaction to the visit. If the one who greets them responds to the request to share their faith the team then proceeds to share Campus Crusade's
"Four Spiritual Laws." This booklet was first revised however, to be
more in line with Chinese thinking. The new title is "The Abundant Life."
After each visitation session, all team members report back to the church;
share their experiences, tabulate the results and plan for the next appointment. Those who made a profession of faith are then revisited when
possible and a special letter of invitation sent inviting them to the
church meetings. Need for Revision: In spite of what appeared to be
highly encouraging results, by the fall of 1975 after one year it had

become obvious that the program was inadequate. Many contacts had been
made; many had heard the Gospel; almost 400 had prayed the prayer of
acceptance but few of them had actually come to church! Further instruction was desperately needed. A more solid foundation had to be
laid before they could expect newly-interested people to come into a
strange church. Adequate bridges between their world and the church
had to be found.

Introduce Home Bible Study

Growing churches are flexible churches. They are not afraid to
try, to fail and to try again. They are willing to honestly evaluate
their results against their efforts. They are willing to change if
their methods do not yield commensurate results. They are always
searching for the most effective methods. They are never satisfied
with the "status-quo."

All of this is true of Freedom Road Baptist Church and their
leader Pastor Hsieh. That is why they grow. The problem mentioned
above had to be faced and resolved as far as possible. The key to the
resolution of the problem was found in a new set of Bible materials
shortly before introduced to Taiwan through the China Home Bible League.
This organization, Taiwan's branch of the World Home Bible League, has
a goal of eventually placing a Bible in every home in the world. In a
few short years they have involved over 10% of the churches in Taiwan
in their Home Bible study program. But few churches put them to better use than the Freedom Road Church. Pastor Hsieh reviewed the materials and found them adequate. Moreover, the C.H.B.L. program allowed the local church to pay but 20% of the cost of materials plus
postage. That amount could be easily handled out of the Evangelism
Committee's budget.

The Bible study program is divided into three parts. Every person
enrolled in the course must begin at the beginning, no matter whether
a grade school graduate, college professor, former Christian or national
assembly delegate - and some of each are enrolled in the current program!
The beginning course has three simple booklets dealing with the basic
concepts of God, man, sin and so on. As each assignment is completed,
it is sent to the church to be corrected. Since its introduction in
January, 1976 a total of 647 students have enrolled and 35% have
graduated. A graduation reward is a book on the life of Jesus.

The intermediate course is more difficult. It consists of a five

book study of the Gospel of John. Within the first year, 133 had completed this level also. (See figure two for a more complete analysis
of results.)

HOME BIBLE STUDY RESULTS - 1976

		Beginning	Intermediate	Advanced
I.	TOTAL ENROLLED	647	272	124
	Male	315	135	73
	Female	332	137	51
	Percentage graduated:	35%	49%	51%
II.	AGE BACKGROUND			
	11-20	67%	47%	22%
	21-30	22%	16%	21%
	31-50	6%	29%	39%
	(Balance under 11 or over 50 years of age)			
III.	EDUCATIONAL BACKGROUND			
	Students/teachers ...	87%	88%	84%
	College level ...	3%	6%	18%
	High School level ...	50%	50%	31%
	Junior High level ...	37%	42%	25%
	(Others in vocational-level training, etc.)			
IV.	RELIGIOUS BACKGROUND			
	Protestant	42%		
	Catholic	3%		
	Buddhist	8%		
	No religion	47%		

Figure 2

The advanced level has five more books dealing with basic Christian doctrines of the church. Of 124 enrollees, 63 finished during
the first year, that is, completed the entire three-part series of
study. Their graduation gift is a Bible.

Beginning in 1976, those indicating interest in the Gospel or in
making a profession of faith were further encouraged to sign up for
this free Home Bible study program. Each visit now includes filling
out the information card, sharing of "The Abundant Life" spiritual laws,
distribution of some basic tracts dealing with the Christian life, a
listing of all church activities with an invitation to attend plus an
enrollment card for Home Bible study. It was the introduction of this
last step that provided the needed bridge between the non-Christian
home and the local church.

Upon completion of the whole series, the student, by then fairly
knowledgeable in the basic truths of Christianity is invited to join

a baptismal class. In September, 1976 the first group of ten received
baptism - the first fruits of a new home study program introduced just
nine months before.

The China Home Bible League is not a center to grade or correct
papers. All of this must be done by the local church. The program
stands or falls upon the ability of the local church to properly administer the program. If properly administered, the results can be
impressive. (See Figure three)[6] To resolve the logistics problem
God raised up a retired military brother (Mr. Yu) who volunteered to
give half-days to directing the program. An average of three more
volunteers aid in the correcting of papers and answering questions.
All questions they cannot handle are personally dealt with by Pastor
Hsieh who also serves as the superintendent of the correspondence
school. Students who falter along the way are sent letters of encouragement and a careful record is maintained of each enrollee's progress.
Interest in the program soon spread beyond the immediate neighborhood.
Friends introduced other friends and soon the church had students from
one end of Taiwan to the other including soldiers on the offshore
islands.

Receptivity: Is "Community Evangelism" effective? It is still
too early to evaluate long term results. Figure one gives a partial
answer. From its introduction in the end of 1973 through 1975, baptisms
doubled.[7]

Statistical data from November, 1974 through August, 1976 also reveal some interesting facts about openness to the Gospel. Of a total
of 2,049 contacts made during this period, only 35% indicated no desire
to listen. Another 36% listened to the explanation of the Gospel and
53% of these prayed a prayer of faith. Another 10% already claimed to
be "Christian" - even though many no longer claimed affiliation with a
church.

Of course few of these began to come to church but many of them
are included in the 647 who signed up for the beginning Home Bible study
course during 1976. In the estimation of a few visitation members, perhaps no more than 10% of the contacts actually shut the door on them
without giving them a hearing.

Figure two is very revealing. One church, committed to evangelistic outreach, in a short 12 months has touched 647 people with a Bible
study program. Contrary to popular belief, students are not primarily

female for slightly more than half of them are male. Nor is the program limited to young people. Intermediate and advanced students show
a high percentage in the "over 30" age bracket. Nor is Christianity
the prerogative of the less educated. About one-half of all students
are in or have the equivalent of a high school or college education.
The Freedom Road Baptist Church "community evangelism" program offers
real promise. It should provide much inspiration to struggling
churches elsewhere in Taiwan.

Apart from the receptivity of the outsider, what impact has this
had on the local church? A number of interviews turned up a consistent
testimony. "The day of mass evangelism is over; non-Christians simply
no longer have the time nor interest to come and hear a preacher."
Everyone interviewed was equally excited about this new program. They
all agreed this is the most effective church growth tool they have
ever used. In the words of the director Mr. Yu, "This approach is much
more practical and effective than mass evangelism. In our increasingly
industrialized society, people rarely have 'time' for church meetings.
Literature work is therefore an important tool and an effective way to
reach their hearts. What needs to be stressed in this type of evangelism is meeting the people 'where they are', not 'where we are!'"

Mass evangelism, however, has not been totally rejected by Freedom
Road Church. During 1975 and 1976 all such meetings were cancelled.
Their results had not been commensurate with the efforts. But in 1977
they will be re-initiated. In their constant desire to experiment, to ad-
just and to search for better methods, a new program will be introduced
for the coming year. Only two months - during the winter and summer
season - shall be used for outreach. The other two quarters will be used
to revisit those who decided to follow Christ during the previous quarter of outreach. In addition the mass evangelism approach will be re-
introduced but this time with a new objective. It will not be directed
toward "society-at-large," but will seek to attract those involved in
their Home Bible study program. The meetings will attempt to solidify
their convictions and to offer the opportunity to publically decide for
Jesus Christ. It will act as a second bridge between the person contacted and the normal life of the Christian community. It is an experiment that merits close attention.

Another side-benefit of the program has been the rediscovery of
many former Christians who have drifted away from the church. This
is especially true of the mainlander Christians who entered in great

numbers in the 1950's and left in equally high numbers in the 1960's.
Conserving this harvest has always been a challenge. Few of them have
been re-contacted since their separation from the church years ago.

With the immediate neighborhood now thoroughly visited, the members have moved out away from the church. They have also tried un-
structured park evangelism and, in 1976 covered the first high-rise
apartment unit where they made 113 contacts. This type of visitation,
increasingly a challenge to the urban church, required some modifica-
tion. To gain access a religious questionnaire was used. After answering the questions about their religious preferences, the team gently
sought to share their own religious convictions. For reasons not yet
clear, and apparently contrary to popular conviction, results in the
high-rise unit, while claimed to be lower than the response in the
residential area, yet according to figure three are actually a bit
higher. The percentage of each district that made a prayer of faith
ranged from 13% to 29% while those who actually indicated a desire to
continue studying the Christian faith ranged from 8% to a high of 19%
recorded in the high-rise apartment house. Only their experience
with free-lance evangelism in the park was higher, due perhaps to their
selectivity in approaching the young and to the greater difficulty of
refusing a stranger when confronted in public. More research and ex-
perimentation would seem to be in order regarding the receptivity to
the Gospel of high-rise apartment dwellers.

How else can apartment dwellers be reached? Pastor Hsieh finds
only one method to be relatively effective: the use of the appointment.
Members of the church are urged to set up appointments with their
friends or relatives living in high-rise units. Through this personal
introduction a much more satisfactory entry is gained and rapport is
established more quickly.

A SUMMARY OF CHURCH GROWTH FACTORS

"Community Evangelism" alone cannot explain the growth of Freedom
Road Baptist Church. It has been correctly stated that when God wants
to grow a church, He looks first for a man, not a method. A church
that continues to grow when others decline and that directly or indirectly has sent over 60 members into full-time Christian service has
been built on a strong foundation. The chief architect has been Pastor
Hsieh and his competent helpmate, Mrs. Hsieh. The consistency of their

COMMUNITY EVANGELISM RESULTS

	No. Contacts	Area	1	2	3	4
Nov., 1974-						
Jul., 1975	1009	Neighborhood	36%	24%	11%	11%
Feb., 1976	555	New community	48%	22%	13%	9%
Aug., 1976	113	Hi-rise apt.	–	23%	–	19%

1 = Not interested
2 = "Accepted" Gospel
3 = Already believers
4 = Willing to study further

<u>Figure 3</u>

Christian life is born out through their five children. One is a
seminary graduate, another in seminary. A third works for a Christian broadcasting studio.

Other growth factors could be listed as follows:

THE PASTOR

A. Has a burden for preaching. Pastor Hsieh sees this as a
basic prerequisite to the success of any program. His people are
well grounded in the Word. Every two years he preaches a complete
cycle of sermons from Genesis to Revelation.

B. Strong leadership is offered with the expectation that the
congregation will support him. Deacons and elders give full support
but are always first consulted. Their approval, based on the pastor's
ability to lead them, is basic to the launching of any new program.

C. An optimistic, positive attitude is displayed. Sharing the
Gospel is not a burden; the Lord's work is not a sacrifice. Pastor
Hsieh wisely refrains from pleading with his parishoners to join the
community evangelism program. They are made to feel it is a privilege
to join. Only those desiring to share in this special blessing can be
used.

D. A keen awareness of the importance of total lay involvement
coupled with the ability to inspire and to train them for service. A
desire to "mobilize the laity" is found in many churches. Pastor
Hsieh goes beyond this by offering clear scriptural teaching on the
basis for total lay involvement plus concrete programs of service for
developing their abilities.

A. Church leaders have refused to limit themselves to methods that no longer produce growth. It would be easy to continue the traditional "evangelistic rally" regardless of results. But results were increasingly meager. The new vision shared from "Explo '74" was but another fresh beginning. Only by testing, by trial and by constant revision did the vision begin to mature and to bear fruit.

B. The willingness to become involved in long-range evangelistic programs. Short-term programs never bear lasting results. Only sustained programs produce sustained results. The church does not readily give up or tire. The program however must be realistic - demanding but not over-demanding, challenging but not exhausting.

C. The congregation WANTS to move out and share the Gospel. This is central. Without this desire to share, there can be no effective evangelism or church growth. A people not gripped by Christ's love will have no motivation for sharing Him. Freedom Road Church members want to share their faith.

D. Opportunities are allowed for mutual upbuilding. Figure one confirms Pastor Hsieh's theory that when people are mobilized for outreach, they themselves are also built up and baptisms increase, not just because of the addition of outsiders but because the members are also more attentive to the unbaptized "inquirers" already within their midst.. It is in the small group that participation is highest and the most intimate, personal fellowship is experienced. Women meet weekly at the church but once a month they meet in ten small groups throughout the city. The men also divide once monthly into six small groups. Attendance usually doubles at these meetings. Opinion seems to favor this type of meeting for its intimate fellowship and opportunities provide for sharing and encouraging. Once a month wives and husbands also meet together.

E. Many types of meetings are held in the church and in the home to meet the various needs of the people.

F. Members are challenged to sacrifice their time and to give of their goods. Because the church was blessed with early independence from mission subsidy, it quickly learned to depend on the Lord for its financial needs. (See figure one.) Many members of Freedom Road Baptist Church have long been willing to follow Jesus' admonition - they have invested both their treasures and their hearts in His church.

G. Unity of spirit and submission to spiritual authority. A
willingness to submit to the leadership of the pastor is essential
if a church is to grow. This means authority must be exercized by
example and not by committee. As the members recognize the spiritual
example of their pastor, as they receive wise guidance and sound
teaching, they submit themselves to his counsel. Pastor Hsieh at-
tributes their unity and harmony to deep spiritual maturity. Others
prefer to attribute it to sound Biblical teaching and an inspiring
example.

THE PROGRAM

A. Clear-cut goals and objectives. Freedom Road Church knows
that all the inspiration in the world is of little avail if it is not
directed toward specific goals. Likewise programs and techniques are
worthless unless the church knows exactly what it wants to do or where
it wants to go.

B. A clear understanding of priorities. Goals must be sorted
out. A church can can get lost in a plethora of goals. Freedom Road
Church programs are directed toward specific goals according to their
importance. Evangelism and church growth are at the head of their list.
Many of their energies are directed toward attaining these goals.
They know what is most important and what is next in importance. That
is an important basic reason for their growth.

But perhaps the final qualities are most difficult to define or
reproduce. Jesus spoke of them frequently. Paul called them "the
fruits of the Spirit." The members of Freedom Road Baptist Church
describe them as "a love for one another." This is especially evident
when they divide into their many small groups. The basis for this understanding - some pointed out - is first learned through the example
of their leader. This love means a love for one another, a love for
sharing the Good News, a desire to see others share in this "abundant
life." "Concern" is the way one member described it. "Prayer" is
what another said was the cornerstone of their growth.

All of these, in varying degrees, can be found in this church.
And so the Lord blesses their life and they grow. And that is what
the Freedom Road Baptist Church is all about.

FOOTNOTES

1. Christianity never exceeded 1% of the population on the mainland although more than 1% of the refugees to Taiwan were Christian. Of the approximate one-and-one-half million who fled to Taiwan, an estimated 10% were Christian by the mid-1960's. It is uncertain whether the figure is still as high due to many reversions.

2. A free translation from the 20th Anniversary booklet of the church published May, 1972. Pg. 7 (Chung-hua Jidujyau Taichung Jinsyin hwei Chengli 20 Jou Nyan Jinyan Tekan).

3. Most mainlanders in Taiwan are found in education, government and the military. The land is primarily owned by the Taiwanese community and most private business enterprises are also under their control.

4. A word is necessary to explain the rapid decrease in baptisms from the year 1960-1962. Prior to that time, church polity required all converts in all the newly established daughter churches to be baptized in the mother church. As of 1960 a number of these chapels became independent churches and their converts no longer had their baptisms administered or recorded in the mother church.

5. Experience seems to show that when a church desires to mobilize the laity for outreach, a 10% response is normal for long-range programs. This church had 591 recorded members for 1976 and an average of 300 on Sunday morning. This is "average" for a growing, healthy church. (See also: C. Peter Wagner, "Seven Signs of a Vital, Healthy Church" Regal Press, Pg. 77F.)

6. John 13:17

7. A word of explanation is necessary regarding figure three. Although a high percentage of students list their occupation as "student" this actually also includes a large number of people in the teaching profession who, for some reason, were included under "students." Thus the high percentage listed both in the "student" category and the "over 30" category. It would seem that teachers are one of the most responsive segments of society.

8. Baptisms dipped sharply in 1976. Observable reasons are:
a) the church did not place as much stress on the need to be baptized during this year.
b) average baptismal age is during student years and for uncertain reasons several more "groups" of youth came together to receive baptism in the years immediately before 1976 .. perhaps again

related to factor "a".

ABOUT THE AUTHOR

Allen John Swanson, born in 1934, is a native of Minnesota.
In 1962 he and his wife Jean went to Taiwan to serve as missionaries
of the Lutheran Church in America to the Taiwan Lutheran Church in
the areas of congregational, youth and university ministries. In 1968
he received an M.A. in Missiology from the Institute of Church Growth,
Fuller Theological Seminary, Pasadena, California. His revised thesis
was published under the title: "Taiwan: Mainline versus Independent
Church Growth." (William Carey Library) Together with Dr. Alan Gates
and Rev. David Liao, he helped found the Taiwan Church Growth Society
in 1971. Since then his articles have often appeared in the Society
bulletin and other mission-related magazines. In 1969 a series of
seven articles based on his original Master's thesis appeared in his
denominational mission magazine "World Encounter" and received the
Associated Church Press award as "the best series of articles in the
field of mission magazines" for 1969.

Since 1975 Swanson has served as Chairman, Division of Mission
in the interdenominational China Evangelical Seminary, Taipei.

Chapter 7

The Sin-heng Church

THE SIN-HENG CHURCH OF KAOHSIUNG
MOTHER OF CHURCHES, ORGANIZED FOR FRUITFUL ACTION

INTRODUCTION

The Sin-heng Church is located in the bustling, industrial port city of Kaohsiung on the west coast of south Taiwan. This city of already more than one million souls is the hub city of the South and is still building and growing. Sin-heng - a member congregation of the Presbyterian Church in Taiwan - is an urban church situated close to the main point of entry into the city - the Kaohsiung Railroad Station. The membership of the church is Minnan Chinese.

DESCRIPTION

A. Historical Background: The church, started almost 40 years ago, was not originally located in the Sin-heng district, but in one of the districts zoned industrial, to the south. In two of these districts - Leng Nga Liau and Chian Tin - there were Christians working in the factories. In order to worship the Lord, a person had to walk a long way to the nearest church, in a district north and west of his home. It was too far for many and they stopped going to church.

In 1938 two laymen and a pastor decided to do something about
this. The pastor was the redoubtable late Rev. Liau Tek who used to
go everywhere preaching the Gospel. The three did not get to carry
out their plan without a struggle, however.

There was a high-ranking leader in Buddhist-Taoist circles named
Siat Beng who, though very familiar with the New Testament, was an
advocate of comparing the five religions together. When he heard
that a Christian chapel was to be started, he sought to lead a crowd
to obstruct it. But Pastor Liau had a fabulous reputation as a de-
bater. He engaged Siat many times in debate and defeated him. So
the obstruction did not take place. The Holy Spirit had overcome
Satan. Siat said, "If we want to preach Taoism, we must do so in
the Christian spirit of Pastor Liau."

On March 12, Pastor Liau and the two elders gathered others together and started the Chian Kim chapel. More than 30 adults and
children attended worship that day. The offering was only two Old
Taiwan dollars. The following Sunday both statistics doubled, showing 100% growth. The church has been self-supporting from the start.

Early in 1940, the chapel was organized as a congregation by
Kaohsiung Presbytery. In that year and the next two it had these
firsts: first communion service with 54 communicants, first elders
and deacons elected and installed, first preacher called. But at
the end of 1943 - due to the especially heavy allied bombing of
Kaohsiung - they were forced by government order to suspend services.
They did not meet again until after VJ day, in the early Fall of 1945.

On May 5, 1946, the moderator of Kaohsiung Presbytery called a
meeting of those concerned and it was decided to move the congregation
and allow Chian Kim to establish another one: the Chian Kim Church,
whose edifice is now a landmark in Kaohsiung. The church moved to
Ming-hsing Street in the northern part of Sin-heng District, to the
home of one of the two elders who had initiated the work in 1938.

For the first ten years of its history, the Sin-heng church was
a house church that met successively in the homes of five different
members. In 1947, when inflation was rampant, they decided to use
five million Old Taiwan dollars to erect a church building. A year
later, on October 3, 1948, the first services were held in the new
building, where they have continued ever since.

Sin-heng church had a total of three regular preachers during

its history. The first one was not ordained and did not return after
the war-time dispersion. The second, installed in 1948 shortly after
the new building was occupied, remained for slightly more than 4 years.
The third - the Rev. So Thian-beng - came early in 1954 and has continued until today.

B. Introductory description of why Sin-heng church merits
special study.

The Sin-heng church is eminently qualified as a subject for church
growth study. It has actively engaged in evangelism and has experienced
Internal, Expansion, and Extension Growth.

> Type 1. It has had Internal Growth in the spiritual growth of
> its members (quality growth) and the structural growth of the
> congregation. This type of growth also includes, not only the
> conversion of nominal Christians within its membership, but
> biological and transfer growth as well.
>
> Type 2. Sin-heng church has undergone Expansion Growth. It
> has reached beyond its membership and engaged in outreach evan-
> gelism. The results are known as conversion growth.
>
> Type 3. Extension Growth is "church planting." The Sin-heng
> church has planted a number of daughter churches and had a part
> in planting more than a dozen more. Its pastor was one of the
> initiators in 1954 of the "Double the Churches" movement (PKU).
> In 1959, Kaohsiung Presbytery, of which Sin-heng was then a
> member church, was the first such district body to attain the
> goal of doubling its churches, a target for its 100th anniver-
> sary in 1965, that the General Assembly had only that year
> adopted for the whole church. Thus Sin-heng church has been
> involved in Extension Growth from early in its history.

The growth of Sin-heng church and the dynamics of its growth are
studies exceedingly instructive and profitable.

E. Statistical Description of the Growth of Sin-heng Church.

We here present four charts which illustrate the statistical
growth of Sin-heng church. As in the increase in weight and height
of a growing child, many aspects of church growth may be measured and
charted. Though there are some aspects of spiritual growth that cannot be thus measured and portrayed, there are others that can be shown.
We make this description:

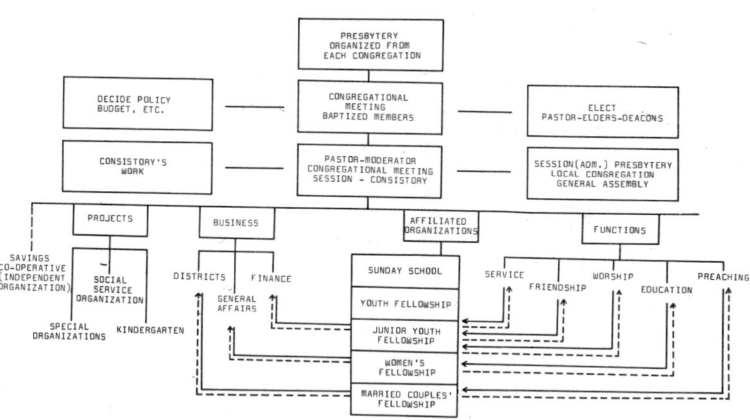


```
FUNCTIONAL COMMITTES:  Preaching  - Evangelism committee, visitation,
                                    literature evangelism, personal
                                    evangelism
                       Education  - Faith & life education, student
                                    scholarship & aid fund
                       Worship    - Ushering, choirs, family worship,
                                    prayer meetings
                       Friend-    - Believers' fellowship, social
                       ship         friendship, youth marriage coun-
                                    selling
                       Service    - Funerals & weddings, charity at
                                    home & abroad, reception of guests,
                                    cemetery, church celebrations

BUSINESS COMMITTEES:   Finance    - Running expenses, building fund,
                                    approve receipts & expenditures,
                                    budget, accountant & cashier,
                                    statistical reports
                       General    - Edit & print weekly bulletin,
                       Affairs      receive & issue documents, compile
                                    records & roll of members, edit &
                                    print schedule of church work,
                                    public relations, record resolu-
                                    tions, repairs
                       Church     - Distributing weekly bulletin,
                       Districts    offerings, other distributing &
                                    contacting, family prayer meetings

PROJECTS:  Kindergarten - "Let the little children come unto me."
                                                        (MT 19:14)
           Social Service Organization - "Healing every kind of
                                    disease & sickness."
                                                        (MT 9:35)
           Special Organizations - Short or long term, unaffiliated
                                    with established organizations.
```

CHART TWO

KAOHSIUNG SIN-HENG CHURCH

1947-1976

Date	Commu- nity	En- quirers	Communicant Members	Adult Baptisms	Bapt. Conf.	Child'n Christ	Baptized Children
1948:	240	105	71	-	-		64
1950:	328	112	126	-	-		90
1952:	653	341	188	-	-		124
1954:	908	500	259	48	6		149
1956:	1126	603	317	51	3		206
1958:	1399	766	363	49	5		270
1960:	1545	821	414	41	9		310
1962:	1515	824	391	35	8		300
1964:	1360	626	424	76	20		310
1966:	1096	519	357	43	6		220
1968:	1553	905	390	53	18		258
1970:	1491	874	385	55	22		232
1972:	1452	847	380	54	16		225
1974:	1013	250	389	60	28		374
1976:	1007	136	524	81	14		347

CHART THREE

KAOHSIUNG SIN-HENG CHURCH

1956-1976, Per Capita Giving

Date	Average Sunday Attendance Morning & Afternoon	Regular Offerings	Per Capita Giving
1956	566	96,000	170
1958	584	113,000	193
1960	580	175,000	302
1962	572	204,000	357
1964	530	283,000	534
1966	446	322,000	722
1968	461	462,000	1002
1970	423	448,000	1059
1972	400	615,000	1538
1974	379	795,000	2098
1976	424	1,211,000	2856

INTERNAL GROWTH

Growth in giving - charts three and four. Sin-heng church has shown phenomenal growth in the area of giving. This is a form of internal growth which is graphically shown on charts three and four. Chart three shows the per capita giving reckoned from the regular Sunday offerings from 1956 through 1976 and chart four shows the total

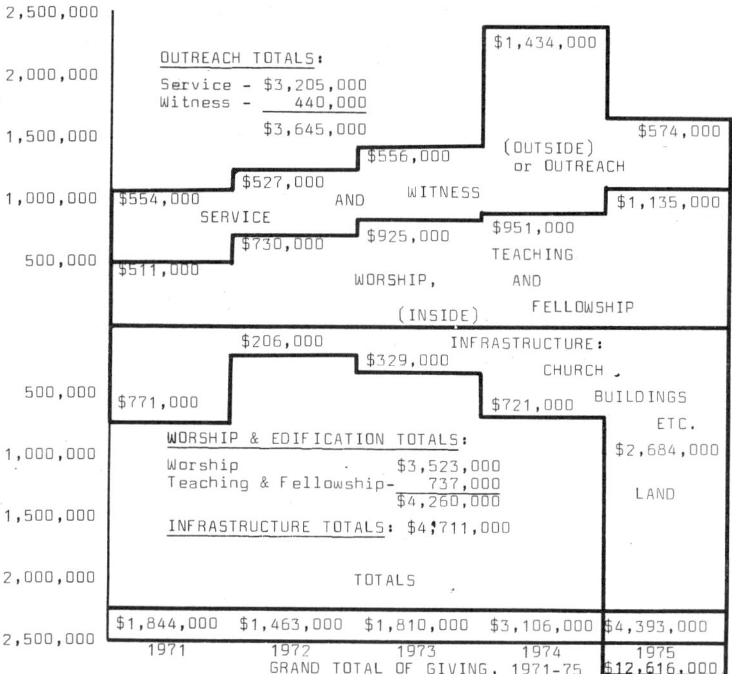

Figures given in local currency.
Divide by 40 to get U.S. dollar equivalent.

giving - both regular and special - for the past five years.

Sin-heng church started out as a house church. Its present
one-story auditorium - erected in 1948 - is actually only adequate as
a meeting place for the congregation as a whole. And yet, from as
early as 1955, it has had 19 or 20 Sunday School classes meeting in
various parts of the building and in adjacent rooms and sheds. Not
until 1970, after over many years raising about NT$1,180,000 to buy
land and buildings for its daughter churches and a residence for its
associate pastor, did the church finally buy, for NT$2,500,000, the
315 ping of land on which it stands. In 1976, it erected and

111

dedicated its modern, four-story educational building at a cost of
NT$4,000,000. In 1975 it had conducted a year-long drive for funds
for the new building. The progress towards the initial goal of
NT$3,000,000 was graphically shown on a thermometer type chart pub-
lished in the weekly church bulletin. At the annual congregational
meeting in January, 1977, a budget of ten million New Taiwan dollars
was adopted for the proposed new church auditorium (architect's sketch
at end of chapter).

Chart three gives the annual average Sunday attendances and the
annual per capita offerings, provides statistics on per capita giving
and its growth. The average per capita increase in regular offerings
from 1956-1966 was NT$55 each, from 1966-1976 NT$213 per year and from
1972-1976 NT$355 every year.

The per capita percentage increase for 1956-1966 was 17% per year;
for 1966-1976, 15% a year; and from 1972-1976 it was 21% a year.

Chart four shows total giving of NT$12,616,000 for the years 1971-
1975 and breaks down as follows:

```
Regular Sunday Offerings:                  NT$3,523,000
Church Committees & Fellowships:               737,000
Outreach:  (Includes:)                       3,645,000
               Social Service -              3,205,000
               Evangelism      -               440,000
Real Estate (land & building):               4,711,000
```

ORGANIC GROWTH

"... Organic growth cannot always be registered statistically,
but it has a physical way of proving its reality. The changing organizational patterns of the church often reflect growth going on ...
Such organic growth may indirectly help statistical growth by providing
new energy or eliminating old obstructions."[3]

The pastor of Sin-heng church, the Rev. So Thian-beng, has a clear
perception of the functions of a congregation of Jesus Christ. As set
forth by the Lord in His Great Commission (MT 28:19,20) and as exempli-
fied by the early church in the book of Acts, these functions are preaching, teaching, worship (prayers), fellowship and service (Acts 2:42-47).
A church cannot grow, says Pastor So, if it loses these functions. So
the Sin-heng church, led by its elders and deacons, has committees and
fellowships to carry them out.

Pastor So also believes that the functional activities are the
responsibility not of one man alone, but of all believers in their

priestly office. They should be carried out throughout the church.

Very early in his ministry Pastor So sought to bring church activities into each household by organizing the church into districts and groups, with each group having an average of 5 households. Later, in 1973, he further developed the church-district-group-household structure into a church-district-family-group-household structure. So now there are 4 districts, 14 families, 48 groups and an average of 5 households to a group. The "Family" unites a number of groups into a close-knit whole.

Sin-heng church is organized for action. Its activities, channeled through some 48 groups, are carried out by 7 committees, 5 fellowships and in 2 projects. Through organization, action is multiplied 50-fold.

Chart one shows the Table of Organization as of 1976. Five of the committees are listed on the right according to the functions they fulfill: preaching, education, worship (prayer), friendship and service, with their several activities below. In the center are the supplementary organizations such as the Sunday School and the four fellowships. Each of the fellowships has its own peculiar contribution to make to the total life of the church.

The Sunday School, in addition to 20 graded classes from kindergarten through adult study class, has a teachers' training class whose personnel changes once a year. This class, taught by the church secretary, has been running for 18 years and there are now more than 300 graduates. The Sunday School also conducts Summer and Winter Bible Schools and encourages its teachers to visit their pupils.

The Junior Youth Fellowship, dormant for many years, was revived in 1968. This was coincident with the total mobilization of the church of 1968 and with the initiating that year of universal education through 9th grade by the government. The youngsters, freed from the inhuman cram sessions prevailing until then, were finally able to turn their attention elsewhere. The Junior Youth Fellowship has a summer conference, especially for the members of Sin-heng church.

The Young People's Fellowship has also, for many years, conducted its own summer conference, separate from joint area-wide or island-wide conferences. Its manifold activities run parallel and are coordinated with those of each of seven major committees of the church. These include the promotion of Bible reading and introduction of Bible

reading methods. In the Fall of 1974, in addition to its diversified
regular weekly meetings and the stated monthly meetings, it started a
Study of the Truth Class on Sunday evenings. It has organized visitation teams; it has conducted three annual Ashrams for youth.

Besides such distaff activities as providing flowers for the
church, cookies for the nursery each Sunday and meals for the regular
recurring retreats and special meetings of the various fellowships,
the Women's Fellowship is most active in Bible study, prayer and evangelism. Its schedule of activities is the most complete of any organization in the church. Nine Bible study cells meet each week in
the four districts and it has organized a number of two-person teams
for visitation evangelism.

The Married Couples' Fellowship was organized on December 14,
1975. Although Sin-heng church has for many years kept statistics on
the number of its families it has averaged 278 for 22 years and two-
thirds of its families are whole unit families. Only with the organization of the married couples has this long latent force been released.
By the nature of its discussions in its first year, it has qualified
as an advocate of Christian principles in the home; by its forming a
choir and engaging in visitation evangelism in the church vicinity,
it has become a new arm of service and witness. It is now in a position to challenge each family to realize its covenant privileges
and responsibilities.

The Worship Committee seeks to promote the daily family altar
and occasional family worship meetings, as well as the weekly prayer
meetings in each of the districts, "families" and groups. Its members
are prepared to lead such meetings when necessary.

The Education Committee, in coordination with the several fellowships, encourages Bible reading and Bible study. For a week at a time
four times a year it promotes a daily early morning Bible study in
the church. It is responsible for preparing enquirers for baptism.

The Preaching Committee uses every means available to promote
evangelism. It especially encourages the organization of visitation
teams by the several fellowships, all who include this in their plans.
Among the many other activities is the evangelistic use of the China
Home Bible League Correspondence course. Emphasis has been on those
within the church; now it is on those without. In 1976, 175   , 175
students were registered. Other notable projects are financial aid.

to small and weak churches and the seasonal distribution of Gospel
tracts at Easter, Mother's Day and Christmas. This is coordinated
with similar activities in the various fellowships. The Committee
Chairman, on a deathbed in Taipei in early April, 1977, had only two
or three requests. Two of them were: 1) Make sure that the Young
People distribute tracts on Easter Sunday as usual. 2) Obtain the
money necessary to fulfill our promise of monthly help to the plains
mountain church in Kaohsiung and to the aboriginal "Water Gate"
student center in Pingtung county.

The church conducts two projects intended for reaching out into
the community. They are: 1) The Kindergarten, established in 1950 and
2) The Social Service Organization, established in 1964. The latter
has maintained a Christian hostel, conducted a church for the blind,
a women's vocational training class and mechanical arts training for
the crippled. Doctors in the congregation take turns in manning a
medical clinic at reduced charges. Other current operations are piano
classes, art classes and flower-arrangement classes.

Members of the congregation are also active in other organizations
serving the public: 1) The Kaohsiung Life Line (1970), though non-
sectarian, has a Board most of whose members are Christian and whose
Chairman is a member of Sin-heng church. 2) The Christian Counselling
Center, established in 1974 by Longevity Mountain Presbytery of which
the church is a member. Members of the church are among those who man
the two phone services of the center: a) the Gospel Line (questions of
faith) and b) the Happiness Line (questions of the family). 3) The Fu
Tse Social Service Center, established in 1975 by a dedicated wealthy
Christian, in which center Sin-heng members are also very active.

The weekly Church Bulletin of six pages is a most important factor
in keeping the wheels of the church organization moving. It is distributed to all households of the congregation by the 48 group leaders
every Saturday afternoon. Besides the order of worship for the next
day's services it contains helps for the daily family altar and for
the weekly sectional prayer meetings, a 1000 word summary of the two
sermons preached the previous Sunday, news and announcements of meetings, and timely articles of interest. In these days, when the work
hours of many prevent them from attending stated church services regularly, the bulletin keeps them in touch, alerts them as to what is
going on and maintains their sense of fellowship. Ten other area

churches have followed Sin-heng in its Saturday afternoon distribution
of the bulletin. It is useful in visitation.

The work of the other committees - Friendship, Service, Finance,
General Affairs and Church Districts - is listed under each committee
on the chart of organization and needs no further explanation.

Good organization opens the way for much activity. But is it
fruitful? At the year's end, there is a review of what has been accomplished and work plans are drawn up for the new year. At one year end,
November 30, 1975, 98 people met together to plan for 1976. As the
pastor says, "If double effort produces half results, there must be
change." So a new start is made each year.

EXPANSION GROWTH

In looking at chart two, we can see the rise in numbers of 1)
community, 2) enquirers, 3) communicant members, and 4) baptized children, over a period of 30 years from 1947 to 1976.

Although there are no records of transfers in and out for most of
these years, the balance between the two is reflected in each of the
four categories. Thus there was a slight drop in each of them in 1961
when 175 people were transferred out to start the An-seng church.
There was a greater drop in 1964 and 1965 when 350 and 150 respectively
were transferred out to start the Tek-seng church. (This is also seen
on chart three.) In the years immediately following each of these
transfers out, viz., in 1962 and 1966, there was a resumption of numerical growth. There was a final drop in 1973 when deadwood of the en-
quirer category was exscinded, in accordance with the disciplinary procedures of Sin-heng church. Apart from these transfers out and the
pruning of the rolls, begun in 1972, there has been constant growth over
the entire 30 years. This has been particularly so since the start of
Pastor So's ministry in 1954. The drops are explained almost completely
by the transfers out and the pruning. Otherwise there has been a steady
climb.

For the period 1954-1976, the average number of enquirers per year
was 649; communicant members, 389; baptized children, 272. A red-letter
year was 1968, when there was a total mobilization of the congregation
throughout the year. In that year the two categories of community and
enquirers reached their zenith for the 30 years of 1553 and 905 respectively. A total of 905 people were enquiring into the Faith during that

year.

Segments 2 and 3 on chart two show average communicant and baptized child membership figures for the years. Segment 2 reflects
Transfer and Conversion growth, and Segment 3 indicates Biological
growth. On the line that separates the two segments are the figures
showing the number of conversions for the years 1954 through 1976.
The figure under the line gives the number of children making their
confession of faith. Subtracting it (6 for 1954) from the figure on
the line (48 for 1954) gives the number of adult baptisms for the year.
The average number of communicant members for the 23 years is 389 and
the average increase by confession of faith is 28, or 7% per year. In
the past 5 years this number increased to 34 by .5%. Conversion Growth
has been slightly more than 7% per year for the whole period, approaching 8% during the last 5 years, 1972-1976.

The aggregate for 1954-1964 of the yearly percentage increase of
baptized children in the Community was 10% or an average yearly increase
of 1%, being much lower than the rule of thumb biological growth figure
of 3%. For the ten years 1964-1974 it was even less, being only 7% or
a yearly increase of .7% baptized children confessing Christ have been
3% of the average baptized child membership during the 23 years. In
the last five years the number confessing Christ has increased to 3%
of the baptized child membership.

EXTENSION GROWTH

We present the chronological table below to show the Extension
Growth of Sin-heng church. Column 1 shows the church mothered or aided
in getting started by Sin-heng. Column 2, the number of people transferred out and column 3, the nature of the help given to a new church.

1	2	3
Liok-hap(1957)	15 families or about 75 people	NT$350,000 given for house & land (1956-59)
An-seng(1961)	35 families or about 175 people	NT$100,000 for house & land (1960)
Tek-seng(1964)	70 families or about 350 people	NT$342,059 for land (1964)
Lo-Nga(1970) (Go Te-chhu)	20 families	
Tiong-seng(1970)	10 families	Financial support for 2 years
Kian-Kang-koe(1970)	5 or 6 families	
Go-Kah(1970)	Leading elder formerly a member of Sin-heng	

Sin-seng(1971)	6 or 7 families	Contributed to rent of meeting place for a period.
Sin-bin(1972)		Bought a house to rent to them. Women's Fellowship gives NT$4,800 a yr.
Tiong-cheng(1972)		Gave NT$1,000.00 per month towards preacher's salary for a year.
Ko-lam(1972)	Preacher a former Sin-heng worker	
Lim-tek(1973)	Preacher a son of Sin-heng church	Preaching Committee's "Evangelism Society" supports this church.
Bin-chok(1973)	15 families, including half of its elders and deacons. The church secretary, Mr. Tan, planted this church and preached here for well over a year.	A former Sin-heng elder contributed NT$400,000.00 to its new 7th floor NT$1,400,000.00 sanctuary.
Thih-lo Sin Chhoan (1975) (Railroad New Village)	One of eight churches started by Longevity Mountain Presbytery in less than 5 years.	Monday evening service led by the Rev. So Thian-beng, Sin-heng's pastor.
Tin-hai(1975)	A church for aboriginal (Paiwan tribe) migrants in Kaohsiung.	Preaching Committee contributes NT$30,000 a year.

In addition, Sin-heng church supports a Paiwan tribe student center in Shui Men (Water Gate) in Pingtung county with NT$30,000 a year. This might be called Bridging Growth or the extending of its witness into another culture. Moreover, since early 1973, Associate pastor Go has been laboring in a Chinese-for-Christ church in Berkeley, California. Though not supported financially by the Sin-heng congregation, his relationship is closer than that of many a foreign missionary to his sending church. Recently he reported that seven doctoral candidates had confessed Christ That is surely Extension Growth.

THE DYNAMICS OF GROWTH

A. Geographical Location and Historical Juncture.

The Sin-heng church is located only two or three city blocks from the Kaohsiung Railroad Station. People moving in from the rural areas to find work in the many factories of the city readily make their way to church. A pastor has described the present historical juncture as follows: "Establishing a city church is like opening a pond. If there is water there'll naturally be fish flowing into it. If there is a church there'll be believers coming to worship." Although this is

somewhat exaggerated it is a fact not easily to be denied that many
village church believers are flowing into the cities and loitering
outside the doors of the churches.

B. The Cultural Ethos.

Why are people attracted to such a church as Sin-heng? They are
attracted to Sin-heng because Sin-heng is a sub-cultural homogeneous
unit composed exclusively of Minnan Chinese. In all the meetings and
services, the Minnan dialect is used. People from the rural churches
of Taiwan at once feel at home in Sin-heng church. Sin-heng people love
to sing and excel at it. The church has four choirs: The regular adult
choir, the Women's Fellowship choir, the Junior Youth choir and the
Married Couples' choir. People from the country also love to sing.
Many years ago two missionary ladies, Mrs. Wm. Gauld, the wife of
George Leslie Mackay's successor in the North and, in the South, Mrs.
W.E. Montgomery, wife of the last principal of Tainan Seminary before
the modern era, taught music to several generations of middle school
and theological students north and south. They are known as "the
mothers of music" in the Church of Formosa.[5]

Country people also find people of their own economic level at
Sin-heng. More than 20 years ago there were 22 professionals and
business executives, 52 artisans, mechanics, mill-foremen and truck
drivers, and 40 unskilled laborers in the congregation. Today that
has changed somewhat. There are now not many poor. But the economic
composition is about what it has always been.

They find people of their own religious background and educational level. About two-thirds of the people are also from country churches.
One-third are new Christians, mostly converts from folk religion. The
people over 50 are primary school graduates. Everyone else has had at
least a high school education.

Another feature at Sin-heng that migrants find familiar and that
has made a contribution to church growth is the hours of Sunday worship:
10 o'clock in the morning and 2:30 or 3 o'clock in the afternoon. This
was necessary in the old days when distances to walk were long and it
was customary to eat your lunch in the church after the morning service
and then make the long walk home at the end of worship in the afternoon. Now no longer necessary, the timetable is still retained in many
Kaohsiung churches. It allows for prayer meetings, Bible classes,
meetings of the session and special meetings at other times on Sunday

afternoon and evening that might otherwise not find a place during
the week in the tight schedules of today.

How does Sin-heng's growth compare with other churches of similar
contexts in the area? Other Kaohsiung churches of the same cultural
ethos have also enjoyed rapid growth at the beginning of their history.
Four churches closely associated with Sin-heng have made good progress.
Starting from scratch, with no financial resources at the outset, Go-
kah had more than 30 people worshiping within half a year; Go-te-chhu
(Lo-nga) had 70; Tiong-seng, more than 80; and Kian Kang-koe had 60 or
70 worshipers after only two months. The average total Sunday attendance of mission-subsidized Sin-ai Reformed Presbyterian Church increased
from 24 to 112 in $3\frac{1}{2}$ years.

C. Communication of Intense Belief in Christ.

Dr. Donald A. MacGavran has noted that "the prime ingredient in
the patristic capture of the great cities of the ancient world was an
intense, fervent faith." He has advocated the communication of such a
faith as one of eight keys to church growth in cities.[6] The attainment
of that goal helps to forge three others of the keys, viz., the sur-
mounting of the property barrier in the emphasizing of house churches,
and the development of unpaid lay leaders.

To inculcate an ardent faith in Christ, one must faithfully pro-
claim Christ in all the Scriptures, for "Faith comes from hearing and
hearing by the word of Christ" (Rom. 10:17). One must have a strong
conviction of the authority and integrity of the entire Word of God.
Such a conviction and such a faithfulness are characteristic of pastor
So's preaching and teaching. An examination of the printed, detailed
outlines of his sermons for the past five years shows this very clearly.

The sermons consist of Bible exposition and the preaching of the
doctrines of the church. There were 20 sermons on Genesis in 1972, and,
in that and the following year, 30 on First Peter. Also in 1973, Pastor
So preached 19 times from the Book of Proverbs.

Beginning with the afternoon service of February 10, 1974, and
continuing in the afternoons throughout 1974, 1975 and into 1976,
Pastor So preached a series of sermons on the doctrines of the church.
For 16 months, through mid-June, 1975, he preached 52 sermons based on
the Westminster Confession of Faith. From then on and well into 1976,
he preached 22 sermons on Angels, Satan and the Last Things.

Beginning in March, 1976, and continuing on Sunday afternoons

throughout the year, he gave 32 expositions of Paul's letter to the
Galatians. In the three years there was also much preaching from the
four Gospels: 1974 - 45 times; 1975 - 17 times; 1976 - 32 times.
Pastor So has sought to communicate ardent faith in Christ.

Pastor So has also sought to train all the church members, that
each may fulfill his proper function in all the activities of the
church. There are leaders at all levels, in all areas, led by the
eight elders and eleven deacons. These head up the different committees and assist the pastor in training. Thus, members of the Preaching
Committee give training to new families in the church for periods of 4
to 6 months in Bible reading, in prayer and in the leading of family
worship. The Education Committee not only prepares enquirers for baptism, it also prepared 31 quizzes (published in the bulletin) in coordination with the pastor's Sunday afternoon doctrinal preaching. In
the training of laymen nothing was more effective than the lively
"Church Gospel School" which the pastor, in pre-television days, conducted each summer over a period of four weeks on week-nights for more
than two hours each night. The school naturally divided into two terms
of two weeks each. Following the Pauline pattern, the first term consisted of twelve lessons on the important doctrines; the second twelve
lessons were on the Christian life. There was a daily quiz and the
call of the roll and believers became well-grounded in the faith.

D. Concern for Youth.

It has been said that if you want to know whether a church is
strong or not, you can tell by whether its youth are active or not.
The writer recalls the first time he visited Sin-heng church in the
Fall of 1968. The large number of teenagers and youths in their early
twenties at Sunday morning worship was a thrill to the soul. I also
recall the first time I ever met Pastor So. It was almost 30 years ago,
two years before I came to Taiwan to live. He was then pastor of the
Ku Sia church in Tsoying. It was a hot summer afternoon and the Rev.
Mr. So was diligently teaching primary school boys the Taiwanese ro-
manized. This would enable them to read the entire Bible in a very
short time, a very much shorter time than by learning the Chinese
characters. Such a concern has produced good response.

The Sin-heng youth leaders, however, have been concerned not only
to attract the young people but also to bring them to trust in Christ.
There are two extreme philosophies for working among young people in

the Church on Taiwan. One is that youth meetings and conferences are
for coming together socially and for recreation, with but a modicum of
devotional activity at the outset. The other is that a young people's
meeting must be like a regular church service and a church camp must be
chock-full of spiritual activity, in both instances with everything designed to bring the participants to Christian commitment. Sin-heng's
view is, on the one hand, that a church camp or get-together cannot
compete with its secular equivalent and should not try, and, on the
other, that a high pressure spiritual meeting defeats its own ends by
repelling precisely the young people that are being sought. The Sin-
heng leaders, mindful of their spiritual goals, have sought to present
a unified young people's program in ways as diversely attractive and as
highly efficient as possible. In line with this, Sin-heng for about 20
years has had its own carefully planned summer retreat. To be true to
their trust, the leaders had to have a separate program. It has been
an important factor in the spiritual growth of the young people.

E. Emphasis on the Family.

In his concern for youth, Pastor So does not isolate them from
their families. Rather, they are included in his more comprehensive
concern for the family. As he says, traditional Chinese ethics takes
the family system as basic.

So Pastor So has sought to bring church activities into the home
and family ways into the church.

1. The early Church met in homes. So Pastor So has promoted: a)
Family worship. On a small scale, each family worships together every
day. On a large scale several families worship together regularly.
Family worship helps to Christianize the home. b) Believers' using
church festivals like Easter, Mother's Day and Christmas to invite
their relatives and friends into their homes for tea or a meal. During
this time they may give a short message or testimony. c) Family Gospel
meetings. It is not easy to get an unbeliever to church; it is much
simpler to get them to your home to hear the Gospel. Afterwards, you
can have some tea and cakes to promote friendship, not like the cold-
ness of a church mission where, as soon as the meeting is over, the
people scatter. d) Family prayer meetings. Move the weekly prayer
meeting into the home. To carry out these suggestions, a parish may
be divided into districts, "families," groups and house-holds as Sin-
heng is.

2. Pastor So looks on the church as the household of God. At the
Sunday afternoon service there may be a "birthday greetings period"
during the announcements. In the impersonal society of today's industrialized city, this type of activity serves to arouse concern for one
another, to promote a more close-knit relationship among believers, to
make them better acquainted and to bring about a warm togetherness in
worship.

These ways of involving the family in Christian activity have resulted in not a few web-movements in Sin-heng church. One by one, people of a number of large family connections have been brought to Christ
and joined the fellowship of the church. The Lord too, was pleased, in
this way, to add to the church those who were being saved.

F. Visitation.

As early as 1955, Sin-heng church had Gospel teams to go out and
preach in the streets and visitation teams to go from door-to-door. In
a symposium held five years ago by the leaders of Sin-heng church and
the three daughter churches - Liok-hap, An-seng and Tek-seng - it was
concluded that the most important and most effective evangelistic
method is the mobilization of believers. However, the most essential
work in believers' mobilization is visitation.

Buddhism and Taoism took root in China, not because of the impress-
iveness of their temples, but because Buddhist monks and Taoist priests
and the "three nuns and six professional hags" entered the homes of the
people, chatting cross-legged, discussing their teachings, exercising
calamities by incantation and begging alms. In much the same way
Chinese legends and folk beliefs were spread for thousands of years
among the common folk. The Lord himself gave us this method to pro-
pagate the Gospel in Matt. 10:12 where He says, "Enter the home and
give it your greeting." Later, the apostle Paul, too, went from house-
to-house.

Visitation is all the more important in this industrialized society
when people often cannot attend church at the stated times and feel iso-
lated and lonely. The Chinese today still like to talk about their problems and they have an avid interest in counselling. Witness the beautiful girls crowding around fortune-tellers' booths in the night markets and the large number of "great soothsayer" ads appearing daily in
the newspapers.

The Sin-heng congregation has exploited this felt need of their

fellow nationals in the interests of the Gospel. Not only have they
been told they should all engage in visitation, they have also been
taught how: visitation should be in pairs; there should be preparation,
the most important of which is adequate prayer. There should be some
knowledge of the one to be visited, whether believer or non-believer;
about when you should call, how long you should stay, what you should
and should not say. They have been trained well and the Lord has
blessed.

G. The Believers' Mobilization of 1968.

After a spiritual retreat early in 1968, the consistory decided to
engage in a mobilization of believers for the entire year, under the
leadership of the pastor in cooperation with Overseas Crusades. The
plan was to mobilize all believers, whether male, female, old or young.
Before getting under way there were six days of early morning prayer
meetings in the church. The efforts of the year were divided into four
periods: January through March, April through June, July through September and October through December, each period having its particular
emphasis. In the first half year much training went on; in the latter
half, there was study and appraisal of the effort.

In the first period there was concentration on "seeking the lost
sheep of the house of Israel." Since it was February and winter vaca-
tion, all could take part, adults, youths and children. There was much
calling on the non-Christian members of partly-Christian families and
those who had not been in church for a long time. Sunday School attendance increased greatly and total Sunday worship attendance rose to 654.
The high point was reached during a week in March when there was day-
time visitation in homes and, on three evenings, cottage Gospel meetings, conducted in four homes of good Christian witness in each of the
districts. There were 30 or 40 present at each place; the atmosphere
was relaxed and happy and the response was good. Results of the first
period were the best of the whole year.

The emphasis of the second period was on cottage prayer meetings
and the visitation of unbelieving relatives and friends. Three days
of these meetings were held in eleven different homes, with nearby believers attending and the elders and deacons leading. During one week,
people were called on whose names and addresses had been handed in by
their Christian relatives and friends. In addition, there were two
district-wide distributions of Gospel tracts, each time 50,000, or the

number of households in Sin-heng district. The climax was reached
during the week of June 9-16, when for five days believers went calling. On two evenings they took those they had called on to one of
four cottage Gospel meetings. On the next two evenings, after the
strangeness had worn off, they took them to meetings in the church.

Highlights in the third period (July through September) were the
mobilization of youth and of medical service.

First was the Young People's summer conference, at which practically all the leaders were young people themselves leading the group
Bible classes. Although only 40 attended, one quarter of them wept as
they testified in repentance of their sins. The Jr. Youth camp, immediately following, was led entirely by young people; there were no
major speakers and all the group Bible classes were led by twenty-year-
olds. Immediately following that was visitation, during which more than
300 youths, who had not attended church or fellowship, were called on.
After three days of visitation there were three days of youth evangelistic meetings. These had been preceded by five days of children's
Gospel meetings at which the evangelists and the workers were all young
people. These were fine examples of youth mobilization.

Entering into September, there was first a period of analysis and
then a week of study and discussion, training and prayer. Then from
September 23-28, there was a week of medical service unprecedented for
a local church in all the more than 100 years of missionary work on
Taiwan. Two thousand five hundred patients from more than 100 churches
in Tainan, Pingtung and Kaohsiung counties came. There were nearly 100
believers, including medical students, nurses and doctors, forming the
largest number mobilized at any one time during the year.

The last period (October through December) was one of assessment
and for the making of long-range plans. December is always the climax
of the church year. First, from the 19th through the 21st were three
days of meetings for cultivating spiritual life. Then on the 22nd,
Christmas cottage Gospel meetings were conducted in which the church's
Christmas activities were moved into the home. These Christmas meetings
were held in five different homes and were attended by a total of more
than 200 people, both Christians and non-Christians.

It may be asked what were the overall results in church growth of
total mobilization. That might be hard to assess, although there are
some statistics to help us.

In the first twenty-one years of the church's history there was a total of 360 confessions of faith (conversions), or an average of 17 per year. In the last nine years since 1968 there were 283 confessions of faith, or an average of 31 per year - an increase of 82%. In addition, members have grown spiritually in that they have learned how to witness and to do personal work among their neighbors.

H. Church Giving and Finance.

What accounts for the phenomenal increase in per capita giving in the Sin-heng church? Chart three shows that the church continued its upward rise in giving until 1968 and then began to skyrocket after 1970.

Someone has said that the strength of a church is not to be seen in the splendor of its building but in the amount of its giving outside its walls. Sin-heng church has long been content with a very ordinary church auditorium, but has given generously to help churches and projects outside. As chart four shows, in the years 1971-1975, when it had at long last (1970) bought the land under it for NT$2,500,000 and was raising the money for a NT$4,000,000 Educational Building, the church was still giving NT$3,645,000 or 29% of the whole for outreach.

What is the motivation behind this giving? It is not tithing, for many in Sin-heng church do better than that. And, in any event, it is difficult for a businessman, in these uncertain days, to make a pledge in advance on the basis of tithing. He does not know how much he may be making next year.

It is rather the principle of stewardship - that all we have is a trust from the Lord - that motivates many of the people in Sin-heng. Like the Macedonian churches, they have first given themselves to the Lord. They count themselves as placed in trust with the Lord's money. So when they are asked to pledge at the end of each year, they ask themselves how much they are going to invest.

In Sin-heng, as elsewhere, it is not the wealthy that are the most faithful givers. It is often those of very modest means. One such member recently pledged NT$50,000 for the new church sanctuary whose initial budget is NT$10,000,000. When asked how he would redeem this pledge, he replied that he would join a loan association and ask for his share on the first distribution.

As for Sin-heng's concern to reach out with the funds it has, that constraint is based on the conviction that the Lord's money should not be idle and on the Lord's word, "It is more blessed to give than to receive."

All organizations that receive and disburse money at Sin-heng
must have a treasurer, an accountant and a bookkeeper; all transactions
must have their proper voucher and receipt and all accounts must be
submitted to auditing once a year. In the more than thirty years of
its history there has never been the breath of a suspicion of the mis-
handling of funds at Sin-heng. The Lord blesses those that honor Him.

I. Ashrams.

Zeal lags and love grows cold. The Lord has given us the Word, the
Sacraments and Prayer as the means of grace to draw us to Him again. In
the Lord's Supper, especially, we have communion with Christ and with
one another.

In order to give opportunity for a more extended period of fellowship in the Word and prayer, Sin-heng church has, since 1972, conducted
Ashrams. An Ashram is a spiritual retreat that came from India via
Japan. As developed in Taiwan, it may be described as follows: A number of Christians gather together in a quiet place for about 40 hours
to read the Bible, to meditate, to pray and to strengthen one another
in the Lord.

In an Ashram there are individual activities, "family" activities,
and activities of all the participants together. Individual activities
involve meditation on assigned portions of the Word of God - each time
two or three chapters in sequence - at three scheduled times, each an
hour in length. Everyone also is to go into the prayer room for individual prayer, an hour at a time. There is a roster where one signs up.
All the hours having been signed for, a chain of prayer is thereby established for the duration of the Ashram. There is a book in which to
record matters of prayer.

The "Family" is an important feature of an Ashram. A person is
assigned to a family of nine or ten others. At the first meeting of
a family, the members introduce themselves. After each meditation each
person shares what he has recieved. There is a time when one "opens his
heart" in confession of sin to God and of faults one to another. They
pray together and a permanent relationship is established whereby they
seek to bear one another's burdens.

All the participants attend the opening worship service, and two
other periods in which there is exposition of the Scriptures. There is
usually a single theme for the conference, developed during these three

periods, in general following the assigned Scripture readings. There
are no other messages. Together also, the participants testify as to
what they have received at the Ashram and they consecrate themselves
anew to the Lord. Having fulfilled the requirements, they receive a
new filling of the Holy Spirit.

There is no closing of an Ashram. Rather, the participants separate to their several stations in life to shine as lights in the
world. The family relationships established are lasting.

Various fellowships in and out of the church have had their Ashrams,
the Young People's Fellowship having had three. The best attended of
these was in 1976 when 84 youths of the high school and college level
took part, 16 being from a Tsoying church. In recent years the young
people's Ashram has replaced the regular summer conference. This is
rather remarkable since there are no recreational activities whatever,
other than an afternoon walk. Mr. Tan Seng-cheng, the church secretary,
has led the young people's Ashrams, and others also.

An all-church Ashram, participated in by 60 people, was conducted
during Chinese New Year, 1977, by a minister from Japan. Half of the
elders and deacons attended, as well as the leaders of all the church
fellowships and societies. In the testimony meeting seventeen persons
told of the blessings they had received.

CONTINUATION

Paul enjoins steadfast adherence to what has been learned and as-
serts as the ultimate ground of assurance that all Scriptures are authoritative and true, which is because they are God-breathed (II Tim.
3:14,16). There can be no continuing loyalty to the Christ of the Word
unless there is loyalty to all the Word of Christ.

People at Sin-heng are apprehensive about the future when Pastor
So will have completed his ministry. Who will succeed him? When former associate Pastor Go returned in the summer of 1975, he had undergone
a transforming change. No longer concerned to be a proper churchman,
but rather a warmhearted pastor with a passion for the salvation and
nurture of souls, he took a stand for the faith of the evangelical fun-
damentalists. But Pastor Go is committed to his work in Berkeley,
which is being greatly blessed of God.

The Taiwan Presbyterian Church is not what it was thirty years ago.
There are new winds of doctrine blowing through the halls of its two

theological schools. From where will there come a successor who will
enjoin the people to ask for the old paths where the good way is, that
they may walk in it and find rest for their souls (Jeremiah 6:16)?

In 1968 some ministers and leaders of Kaohsiung Presbytery became
deeply concerned about the secularization of the Church. They organized
the Calvin Study Society which they described as a Christian learning
and study organization with the purpose of reviving the faith of the
early Church by studying and putting into practice the spirit of Calvin.

The same leaders found a deep-reaching cleavage in spirit, polity
and principle within Kaohsiung Presbytery. In 1972 they petitioned for
the establishment of a new presbytery within the same geographical area
as Kaohsiung Presbytery. The General Assembly granted their request and
constituted Longevity Mountain Presbytery on July 4, 1972. Freed of the
evils of contention and divided counsels, this new Presbytery has forged
ahead. Early it set as its goal the establishment of ten house churches
within Kaohsiung county and city. Less than a year after organization
it had already established seven. Longevity Mountain Presbytery now has
37 churches; Kaohsiung Presbytery has 47.

Members of Sin-heng church were constrained to have separate young
people's retreats. They were active in the starting of a separate Presbytery. Do they and other churches of like faith have a source of ministers who will maintain the continuity of their witness?

FOOTNOTES

Note: Most of the information in the report is derived from the
             following sources:

             Sin-heng church secretary C.S. Tan's "An Analytical View
             of Evangelism in the Taiwan Church"
             Handbooks for congregational meetings (1955, 1958, 1974,
             1975, 1976, 1977) of Sin-heng church
             Bound church bulletins (1972-1976) of Sin-heng church

REFERENCES

1. Committee, 1977, p. 164;
2. Yang, 1976, pp. 5,6;
3. Tippett, 1967, p. 31;
4. Tan, 1972, pp. 36, 37;
5. MacMillan, 1963, p. 83;
6. McGavran, 1970, p. 292.

BIBLIOGRAPHY

MacMillan, Hugh, First Century in Formosa, China Sunday School
   Association, Taipei, 1963.

McGavran, Donald A. Understanding Church Growth, Wm. B. Eerdmans
   Publishing Co., Grand Rapids, 1970.

Tan, S.C. "An Analytical View of Evangelism in the Taiwan Church,"
   Church Gazette Corporation, Tainan, 1972.

Tippett, A.R. Solomon Islands Christianity, Friendship Press,
   New York, 1967.

Yang, Bill T.C. Basic Principles of Missiology, Taiwan Church
   Growth Society, Taichung, 1976.

ABOUT THE AUTHOR

Egbert W. Andrews (66). Orthodox Presbyterian Church, Committee
   on Foreign Missions. Became resident missionary in Taiwan, February 23, 1950.

Taipei: 1950-67. Engaged in student evangelism while teaching
        English in the National Taiwan University, 1950-53; In
        Tankang College of Arts and Science, 1953-61; Taught
        Old Testament studies at Taiwan Theological College,
        Taipei, 1962-65; At Calvin United Theological College,
        Hsinchu, 1965-66; Engaged in church planting in Taipei,
        1953-65.

Kaohsiung: 1968-77. Engaged in church planting and theological
        education: resident, Hsinchu, 1968-69; TEE, Kaohsiung,
        1974-75; Chaochow, 1976; Taipei, extension, 1977.

Chapter 8

THE T'UNG-HWA CHURCH OF KEELUNG:

A CHURCH THAT SOWED IN TEARS

AND

REAPS WITH SHOUTS OF JOY!

Pastor Hsü

The birth and growth of the T'ung-hwa Church in the harbor city of Keelung is an inspiring instance of how God prepared and called a gifted pastor to be on the spot when a homogeneous unit of humble dock-workers became receptive to the message of the Gospel.

The present church, located in an unpretentious multi-story complex, looks more like a typical Taiwan apartment store building than a church. It stands in the T'ung-hwa Village of Keelung's Chung Shan District. Here over 120 believers gather every Lord's Day to worship God and to hear the Word preached. Before acquiring the present property in 1971, believers worshipped in a humble warehouse.

The T'ung-hwa Christian Church exemplifies unusual church growth. It was founded in 1967 by the Rev. Hsu Hung-jen in an unchurched district. Previously, three other church groups had attempted to start a permanent Christian witness there but had failed. When a people-movement to Christ began to develop Pastor Hsu was on hand and was quick to seize opportunities to plant a church.

Prior to this, Pastor Hsu had been successful in pioneering two churches in Tainan County. In one of these, prayer for the sick and their subsequent healing brought in seven of the 26 families that ultimately came to know the Lord and became members under his leadership.

After much prayer, on March 20, 1966, Pastor Hsu had felt the urge
to move with his family from Tainan County in South Taiwan to Keelung
on the northeast coast. This step of faith led him to settle in a small
rented apartment in the T'ung-hwa Village, trusting God for his needs.
Of the people here, at least 45% were dockhands and another 10%, sailors,
fishermen and day-laborers. Migrants from Miaoli County over 100 milo-
meters away had trekked northeast to find a better life in the city. It
was among a group of about 20 of these families that the T'ung-hwa Church
got its start. Many of them, being illiterate, had had to take the most
menial jobs available. They had settled in makeshift houses on the hillsides. Their move along with poor living conditions had opened them to
change. Previously very idolatrious and strongly superstitious they became receptive to the Gospel message when it was preached in their homes.
Pastor Hsu began immediately to call on these people, showing them love
and concern. He told everyone in his house-by-house visitation that he
was a Christian preacher and wanted to be "a friend of everybody." To
those who had plenty of time on their hands sitting around local Buddhist
temple doors, he talked about Jesus Christ.

After nine months of visitation and preaching, a small group became
inquirers. The first meeting with seven present was held in very humble
circumstances in the sitting room of a Mr. Chen. Mr. Chen, a refugee
from mainland China, was a dockhand in Keelung's busy harbor. Prior to
his coming to Christ he was very fond of gambling. He first heard of
the Gospel when he was in the hospital suffering from a bout of rheuma-
tism. Pastor Hsu prayed for him and he received healing. At times Mr.
Chen felt very homesick and longed to be back in his mainland Chinese
home area. Pastor Hsu witnessed to him concerning a beautiful heavenly
home that would be his one day should he place his faith in the Savior.
Mr. Chen and his family became Christians.

After his conversion Mr. Chen became an earnest witness of the Gospel. To fellow dockhands at the harbor who suffered from sickness and
poverty he talked about Jesus Christ.

One these fellow dockhands was a Mr. Hwang A-shui who lived near
Pastor Hsu's home. It was through Mr. Hwang that the T'ung-hwa Christian Church actually was started. The story is this: Mr. Hwang fell very
ill and was treated at a Christian hospital in Shih-Lin near Taipei. He
was so moved by the "tender heart" of the Taiwanese Christian doctor,
Chang Ming-yueh, that he accepted Christ as his Savior and requested

baptism.

After his baptism, a very strange thing happened. Mr. Hwang said
that he had seen the Lord and that in three days the Lord would receive
him to Himself. He arranged for his return to Keelung and told his wife
that at 4:00 p.m. on the third day he would be received into heaven.
Precisely as he had predicted, Mr. Hwang died at 4:00 p.m. on the third
day just after he had entered into his house.

A Buddhist funeral was arranged for Mr. Hwang. His younger brother,
however, objected. He said that since Mr. Hwang had become a Christian
three days before he died, and had requested this, that the funeral
should be a Christian one. The widow agreed. But they didn't know any
Christians, so who would officiate? Their answer came when Pastor Hsu,
who had heard about the death, came to the family to comfort and to minister to them. They asked him to conduct the funeral. Mrs. Hwang and
her seven children were deeply moved by the funeral message and spontaneously were converted to Christ.

This opened the door for further contacts to this enterprising and
self-sacrificing pastor. Through unceasing visitation and teaching the
Word in homes, the Gospel began to flow along the natural family and
friendship lines among this small homogeneous unit of humble laborers.
Soon a small people-movement was under way. The following chart and
text, first developed by the Rev. Allen Swanson, explains the network
of relationship along which the Gospel flowed in the next few months:

CHART OF FAMILY AND NEIGHBOR CONTACTS

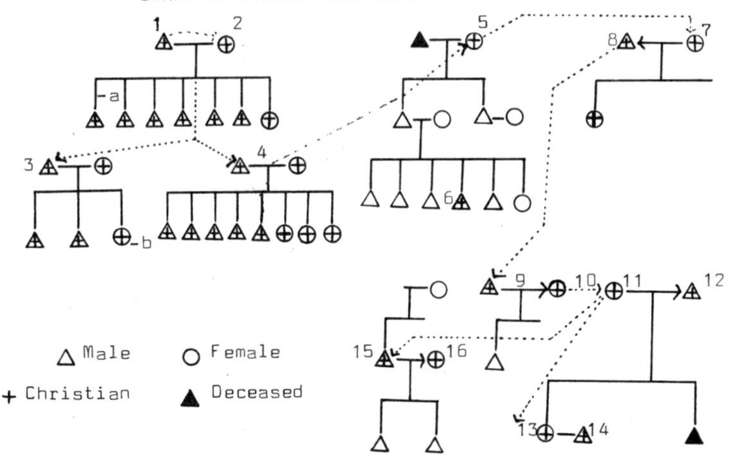

- adapted from Swanson 1971:14-17

133

1. Mr. Hwang died three days after his conversion.
2. Mrs. Hwang, the widow, and all her seven children were led to
    Christ by Pastor Hsu.
    - The oldest son later studied at the Hsinchu Bible Institute
    of the Presbyterian Church of Taiwan and now pastors a church
    in I-nan.
3. A close friend attended Mr. Hwang's funeral. His whole family
    was converted.
    - Now a full-time T'hwa church nursery worker.
4. A very close friend attended Mr. Hwang's funeral. He led his
    entire family to the Christian faith.
5. An old grandmother heard the Gospel in No. 4's home. (Pro-
    bably Pastor Hsu conducted house meetings there). At first
    she opposed the preaching of the Word of God. She suffered
    from a serious internal stomach bleeding. One day she listened
    to the Gospel message and, to Pastor Hsu's surprise and joy,
    she accepted Jesus Christ as Savior. Pastor Hsu prayed for her
    and she was healed. After her conversion at the age of 72,
    she was baptized by Pastor Hsu. She lives with her older son
    and his children, one of whom is also converted.
6. She is closest to this grandson.
7. A former neighbor of No. 5 heard the Gospel. Although she was
    mentally ill for seven years, she, too, was prayed for by
    Pastor Hsu and was healed as well as converted.
8. She then led her husband, a police officer, and their daughter
    to the Lord.
9. A fellow policeman of No. 8 was led to Christ by No. 8.
10. Wife of No.9 was led to Christ by him.
11. A neighbor lady of No.10 was won by No.10. She then was bap-
    tized at the age of 66.
12. The husband of No.11 was converted to Christ.
13. The daughter of No.11 and No.12 was converted to Christ.
14. The daughter's husband whom she brought to Christ.
15. A grandson of No.11 whom she brings to church.
16. Wife of No.15 also believes.

Readers should trace the flow of the Gospel witness within the in-
tricate network of blood-relationships of marriage and family, friend-
ships and neighborhood associations. The following connections are discernable:

Parent to child	.... 19 cases
Husband to wife	.... 5 cases
co-worker to co-worker	.... 3 cases
Woman to woman	.... 3 cases
Wife to husband	.... 3 cases
Grandmother to grandchild	.... 2 cases
Neighbor to neighbor	.... 3 cases

Note that where both the husband and wife believed the Gospel, the entire
family was converted. The graph shows three such cases.

Through the unusual conversion of Mr. Hwang and the profound influence of his Christian funeral, therefore, 34 members of families,
neighbors and friends were brought to conversion and into fellowship

of the T'ung-hwa Christian Church within a relatively short period of time.

As the number of converts grew, they moved into a warehouse belonging to Mrs. Hwang, widow of No.1 in the chart. This building had to be torn down, however, when the Keelung Harbor Bureau widened a road in the area. This emergency forced the young congregation - then numbering 70 by 1972 - to some earnest prayer, fasting and planning. In due time, Pastor Hsu was able to locate a site with an uncompleted building and a church building program was started. As the Lord blessed, the people began giving more and more of their income until the chapel, seating over 100, was completed.

By 1976 the original chapel had been expanded so that the 68 "families" then registered with the T'ung-hwa Church, could worship to-gether. The total adult membership stood at 180 with an average attend-ance of about 130. (See growth graph). The church now has a full-time assistant pastor and also operates Faith-Love Kindergarten with 77 child-ren enrolled.

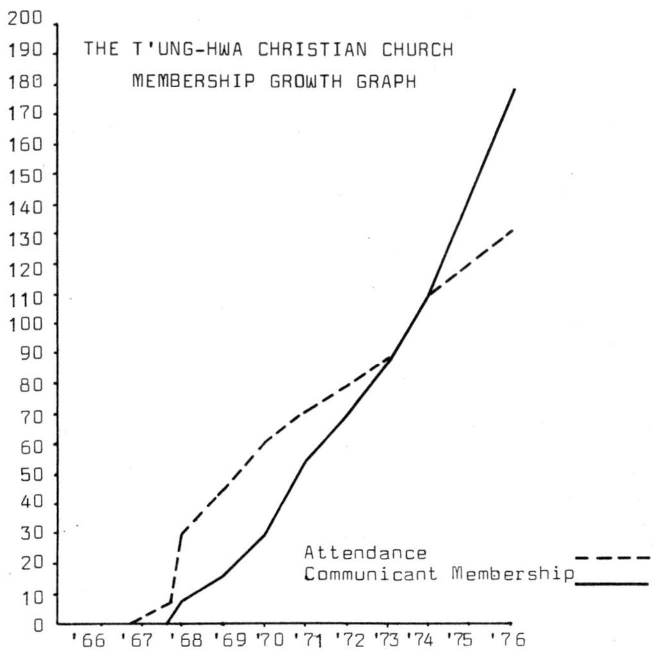

This is good growth for one congregation in the relatively resis-
tant non-Christian province of Taiwan. Pastor Hsu's church-planting
principles are unique and worthy of note; they are not the product of
traditional western church thinking. The following guidelines, initially gleaned by the Rev. Allen Swanson, are what Pastor Hsu has followed in starting and developing the T'ung-hwa Church:

1. Seek out families in need, in trouble or having illness. Counsel
with them and pray for them.

2. Seek out the oldest, the most authoritative figure in the family
and first preach the Gospel to him.

3. Seek out the most superstitious people, as their religious zeal
is a good indication of their devotion. They make the best Christians.
Those who believe nothing before becoming Christians usually make luke-
warm Christians afterwards.

4. Do not emphasize youth work. Youth rarely lead their parents to
Christ. Their conversions often result in rejection or persecution by
their parents, thereby closing the door to future contacts with the
parents.

5. Thoroughly instruct each adult on his or her responsibility to
lead the children to the Lord. If they feel unqualified to witness to
their children, have them bring the children to the church for the pasto
to instruct.

6. Let the decision to follow Christ be a family decision. Do not
obstruct the function of family connections, "the bridges of God," by
ignoring the possibility of the majority's trusting in the Lord.

7. Readiness for baptism is indicated by a willingness to pray
publicly during a worship service, no matter how illiterate the person
may be.

8. All Christians, regardless of how poor they may be, are early
taught the biblical principle of tithing.

9. No household can receive baptism without first publicly destroying all household idols.

10. From conversion onwards, everyone is expected to serve the Lord
and the church in some way. Seven committees, or "teams," exist for the
benefit of every member (adapted from Swanson 1971:13-14).

The seven committees or "teams," each composed of five or six members, are as follows: the Gospel-witnessing Committee, the Prayer Committee, the Visitation Committee, the Finance Committee, the Reception

Committee, the Youth Committee and the Women's Committee. All commit
tees are under the supervision of Pastor Hsu and his Board of Deacons.

The Visitation Committee or Team should be given special attention.
The members of this committee carefully note who are absent in any given
service and then promptly visit the absentees to learn the reason for
their absence. The pastor is then informed of any special circumstances
that should require a pastoral call. Such concern upon the part of the
church for its members prompted one member to exclaim: "The most remarkable characteristic of our church is the mutual love of our people for
each other!"

The T'ung-hwa Christian Church's Gospel Team is actively involved
in the witnessing of Christ's power to save. They sing, they play gui-
tars, they do personal evangelism.

The church now has further outreach through two preaching points.
One is in the home of a new convert, Mr. Lee, who lives in an outlying
area of Keelung where fishermen and miners are being reached with the
Gospel. Another preaching point is on Hsi-ho Street in the home of an
old, as-yet-unconverted man! An average of 20 gather here every Sunday
evening for a worship service.

The Prayer Committee's ministry of intercession is a secret of
growth in this remarkable church. Fasting and prayer take place here
once a month and every two or three months there may be an all-night
season of prayer. One of the "prayer-warriors," a sister, as a result
of combined prayer and fasting in the church, saw a total of 18 members
of her family, children and grandchildren, brought to the Christian faith.

Pastor Hsu's wife is a woman of faith and prayer. During their
early years of pioneering in Keelung, there were times of insufficient
food for the family. Mrs. Hsu, however, always knelt in prayer before
she cooked the food, whether there was little or nothing in the way of
supplies. She and her husband experienced Divine provision for their
needs!

The Finance Committee is linked with one of the reasons for the
success of this church: self-support. From its start Pastor Hsu and his
people have looked to the Lord for the supply of all financial needs.
The people have been taught to tithe their income for God's work. As
a result the financial income of the church has been as spectacular as
the growth in attendance. Offerings for the year 1968 totalled about
NT$6,000, in 1976 the annual total was well over NT$200,000. In five

years they witnessed the Lord's supplying NT$2,000,000 for the various building projects.

Offerings came in from local sources, from other parts of Taiwan and from abroad. An amazing feature is that people normally considered too poor to give have given and have been blessed by the Lord for their gifts!

Bordering the area of supernatural financial provision for this church is also the element of miracles that have turned scores of families from a pagan, idolatrous and superstitious background to a faith in Jesus Christ. Those who migrated to Keelung from Miaoli were known to be idol-worshippers and hard-core animists; they were fervent believers in the world of spirits around them and ardent followers of their Taiwan folk religion. What brought such a round-about turn in their lives?

Some term it the "power encounter." The church is engaged in a spiritual warfare, not a warfare "against" existing cult patterns of the religious and social structure, but rather warfare "within" the cultural patterns. Lurking behind much of the local religious and social structure are opposing demonic forces labeled by Paul the Apostle as "principalities," "powers" and "spiritual hosts of wickedness" (Eph. 6:12).

The power encounter is inevitable. The Early Church recognized the presence of demonic forces, even behind the guise of idols. They exorcized demons in the name of Jesus Christ (Bolton 1976:305).

Pastor Hsu is aware of the spiritual conflict in which he is invovled. References above have been made to his praying for the sick and distressed. Healing and comfort have been the result. In published report of the first five years of T'ung-hwa's history the following episode took place: "Two people were possessed by demons. Pastor Hsu laid his hands on them and in answer to prayer the demons were cast out." In some of the research made on the experiences of new converts, some testified to a dreadful fear of "demons," "evil spirits" and "dead persons" prior to their conversions. Upon their coming to Christ such fears disappeared (Bolton 1976:197-198).

A woman greatly suffered for years from diabetes and paralysis despite much help from doctors. Subsequent to her repentance of sins and conversion to Christ, her sickness was miraculously healed. This moved her husband to accept the Savior. Eight others, family members and neighbors, were converted to Christ as a result of this healing miracle.

According to a survey made by the author, about 40% of the church members were converted to Christ as a result, directly or indirectly, of some miracle. T'ung-hwa Christian Church is a demonstration of the power of the Holy Spirit to meet human need and to draw a people to Christ.

In a recent anniversary report, celebrating five years of progress since the initial building stage of the T'ung-hwa Church in 1972, Pastor Hsu Hung-jen quoted from Psalms 126:5: "May those who sow in tears reap with shouts of joy!" He alluded to the hardships, sacrifices, toil and tears experienced over the years of church-planting. Love's labors were not in vain, for the church experienced also a harvest of souls bringing great joy and victory! Joy because many repented of their sins and victory because many learned to place their trust in an All-powerful Savior!

Pastor Hsu is not resting upon past accomplishments of his T'ung-hwa Church ministry. He further quoted the Apostle Paul, in his fifth anniversary report, as follows:

I am under obligation both to Greeks and to barbarians,
both to the wise and to the foolish: so I am eager to preach the
Gospel to you also ....

Woe to me if I do not preach the Gospel (Rom. 1:14; I Cor. 9:16).
These words give us insights into a Taiwanese pastor s heart, a clue to the burden and passion of a man's life: to win the lost and to uplift the fallen and to place them in a fellowship of a church that is concerned with people!

REFERENCES

BOLTON, Robert J.

1976   Treasure Island: Church Growth Among Taiwan's Urban Minnan Chinese South Pasadena, California, William Carey Library.

1977   "Gathering a People in Taiwan," Church Growth Bulletin, Vol. XIII, No.3:99 - 102.

HSU, Hung-jen

1971   T'ung-hwa Christian Church," Special Church Report, Keelung, Taiwan.

1976   Interview with writers

McGAVRAN, Donald A., WANG, Cheng-chung and GATES, Alan

1976   Church Growth (second Chinese edition). Touliu, Taiwan, Taiwan Conservative Baptism Literature Committee.

SWANSON, Allen J.
1971   "People Movements and the Church in Taiwan," Taichung, Taiwan,
       Church Growth Seminar mimeographed paper.

ABOUT THE AUTHOR

William Luo, Jung-kuang, age 36, serves as assistant pastor of the
Hukuo Presbyterian Church. He is also the General Secretary of the
Hakka Evangelical Missionary Society, an organization dedicated to reach-
ing the ethnic Hakka people with an indigenous expression of the Gospel.
During 1973-1974 Rev. Luo studied at the Andover-Newton Theological
School in the areas of missions and pastoral counselling. He is current
chairman of the Taiwan Church Growth Society.

Chapter 9

THE

BEAUTIFUL

HARBOUR

CHURCH

The Chiangs and Tanks - A Good Team

A CHURCH-PLANTING & CULTIVATING CHURCH

The Mei-kang[1] or "Beautiful Harbour" church belongs to the East
Coast Presbytery of the Taiwan Presbyterian Church. It is situated
in Lower Meilun, a suburb of Hwalien, a city with a population of about
120,000. Hwalien is a county capital and the largest city on Taiwan's
east coast. Mei-kang's membership is predominantly middle-class (See
Chart VI, A,B), but many of its members originally were poor. Ethni-
cally most of them are Taiwanese (Minnan) with a sprinkling of Mainland Chinese and tribal people added through intermarriage with Taiwanese members.

The beautiful, bustling and expanding harbour near which this
church is located may well be a symbol of its life and outreach. Spiritually Mei-kang has "gone out to sea" in at least three major ways: 1)
In its church founding (and "adopting") ministry. Eight "churchlets"
have been founded or adopted by this church, above and beyond its own
full-orbed schedule of Sunday School, youth work, Sunday morning and
evening worship services, prayer meetings, family worship,[2] visitation,
and regular services at a jail and detention home. 2) In its lay mobilization. Of its 109 locally resident members, 69 are zealously active
in church extension, preaching, visitation, personal evangelism, teaching,

serving or leading. 3) In its strong "prayer power" emphasis. A master list of nearly 200 prayer requests is constantly in flux as answers to prayer are written in and new requests added.

The good reports about this church now need to be analyzed in order to separate fact from fancy, history from hearsay, and to sift out the pure gold for the benefit of others and the glory of God. What are the secrets behind Mei-kang's energy and outreach?

AN HISTORICAL SKETCH

Pastor Chiang Tien-sun and his wife have had a church founding vision for years. In fact between 1951 and 1954 three mountain churches were founded near Luo-dung as a direct by-product of their active ministry there. In 1956 they also helped found the Bei-bin Church in Hwalien, but they felt there was great need in Hwalien and along the eastern seaboard for more "plains" people[3] churches.

Their opportunity came when a large public housing project was completed near the Meilun Harbour in 1958. They bought an apartment in the new housing area and began Sunday School and adult meetings in their own home in October of 1960. In spite of opposition, sickness and financial difficulties, attendance at Sunday morning worship services grew from 5 or 6 to around 30 within a year. By July, 1962, the average church and Sunday School attendance had risen to over 40 and 50 respectively, and Mei-kang was officially recognized by the East Coast Presbytery in a dedication service. Severe over-crowding led to the renting of the apartment next door. The wall was partially knocked out between the two apartments and the combined structure was dedicated to the Lord in a thanksgiving service in July of 1963.

A great step of faith was needed to accomplish this much. No official outside financial help was given to this church for rent, pastor's support or operational expenses at any time in its history. The pastor received no salary for almost three years. To pay for the children's education, the newly-bought apartment, and living expenses, he worked hard in his fruit orchard and she part-time as a pharmacist, but in response to Psalm 55:22 they resisted the temptation of full-time secular work even after their fruit business failed. The Lord miraculously supplied all their needs so that later four of their children were able to attend seminary and one, university. But in the meantime she became sick.

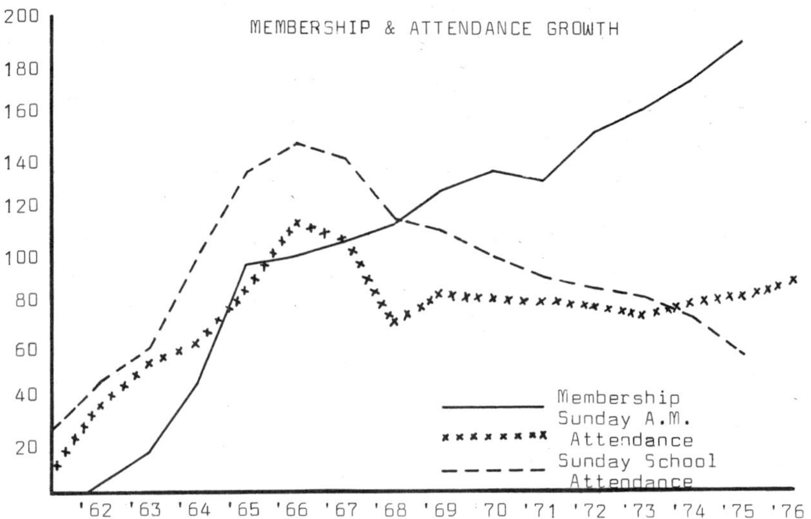

MEMBERSHIP & ATTENDANCE GROWTH
200
180
160
140
120
100
80
60
40
20
Membership
Sunday A.M.
Attendance
Sunday School
Attendance
'62 '63 '64 '65 '66 '67 '68 '69 '70 '71 '72 '73 '74 '75 '76

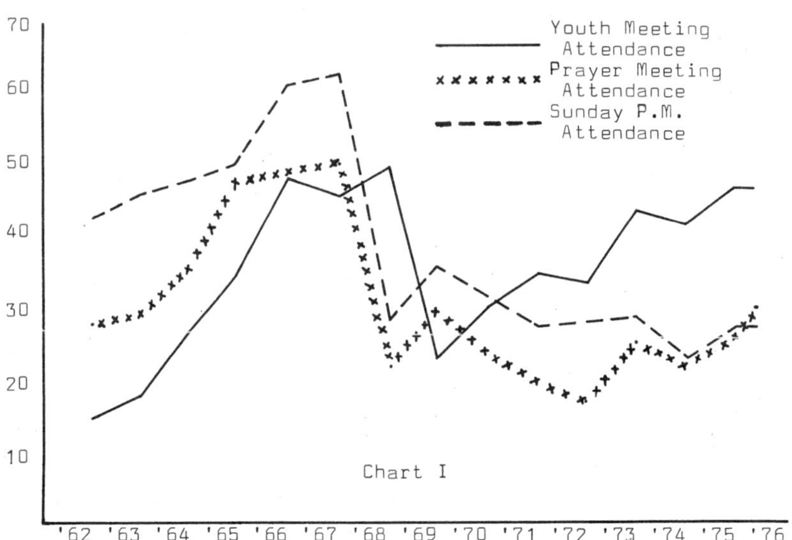

70
60
50
40
30
20
10
Youth Meeting
Attendance
Prayer Meeting
Attendance
Sunday P.M.
Attendance
Chart I
'62 '63 '64 '65 '66 '67 '68 '69 '70 '71 '72 '73 '74 '75 '76

It was during this critical time that the pastor's wife in particular began to pray in a special way. She made a prayer list with specific requests. Four of these were signally answered:

     1) Help the church grow
     2) Find suitable workers
     3) Build a church within $2\frac{1}{2}$ years
     4) Receive healing for her sickness

Quantitative growth proceeded rapidly. By 1965 Sunday School
attendance had risen to 130, Sunday worship attendance to over 80 and
actual adult membership to nearly 100 persons (See Chart I).

More workers were needed. From the original three lay workers the
workforce grew to an impressive number of zealous lay volunteers. But
perhaps most significant of all, in July of 1964, the Vernon Tanks[4], a
Presbyterian-Lutheran missionary family, began to attend their services.
They and their "gospel car" were later to play an important role in an
extensive church founding and servicing ministry.

The two-apartment combination was by now bursting at its seams.
In August of 1964, 300 ping[5] of land were bought near the housing area,
at a time when the government only sold 65 ping plots. In May of 1965
the building of the new chapel was begun, approximately $2\frac{1}{2}$ years after
the prayer request for it was made, and on August 3, 1965, the building
was officially dedicated. The chapel's seating capacity is 200. The
land was paid for in about six months after purchase, and the building
in about one year after completion. Dr. George Hudson, who held two
weeks of evangelistic meetings in connection with the dedication, had
provided U.S.$1000 or NT$45,000 for the building and the East Coast
Presbytery added NT$10,000 toward a total land-building project of over
NT$310,000. The rest was paid for or raised by the members themselves.

Finally, when Mrs. Chiang was about ready to undergo an operation
for her malady, many again prayed for her. Her sickness gradually disappeared and she was spared an operation. She has been well and active
every since.[6] All four major prayer requests were answered.

The pinnacle in Sunday School and church attendance was reached the
year following the church dedication, 1966, after which there was an almost uninterrupted decline in attendance for about seven years. 1966-68
also saw few adult baptisms or confirmations (See Chart II). Reasons for
this decline will be given later. Dissatisfaction with this decline,
however, resulted in two new efforts or ministries.

In the summer of 1969 James Tai of Campus Crusade was invited to

hold a workshop in personal evangelism. Fire caught especially among
the young people. Personal work was done by them almost daily with
patients at Mennonite Christian Hospital and the residents of a large local old folks' home. Moreover, six student Christian fellowships were
started in as many high schools and Mei-kang youth were responsible for
speakers and activities for about two years. That year saw the largest
increase in church membership with a total of 39 persons joining the
church, 27 of them by baptism from non-Christian background (See Chart II).

The second effort began with the return of the Vernon Tanks from a
year of "Church Growth" studies at the Institute of World Mission,
Pasadena. This, together with a readiness for outreach beyond the local
church on the part of Mei-kang leadership, soon resulted in the goal of
"two new 'churchlets' a year." Thus between 1969 and 1975 a total of
eight of these "churchlets" was either taken over from other groups or
founded by the Mei-kang Church (See Chart III). Five were founded by
the Mei-kang workers, three were taken over from other groups and revit-
alized. One of these has since been dropped by Mei-kang since it has its
own pastor. The other seven are regularly visited or served by Mei-kang
workers. Five of the total have Sunday Schools. Three have chapels with
land; four meet in homes. One has bought land. One has nursery and kindergarten work.[7] It might be of interest to note that over 150 adults
meet in these outpost churchlets every week. Together with various types
of meetings in the mother church, a total average attendance of 332 persons per week was recorded for the year 1975.[8] Many of the converts in
the outpost churches are now baptized in the mother church and are considered a part of the total picture of Mei-kang's work and outreach.

Since 1974 two weekly services, one for women, one for men, have
been started at the local jail and six services a month at a detention
home as well. Thus the work goes on and life bursts forth in new direc-
tions.

FACTORS IN THE GROWTH OF THIS CHURCH

We come back again then to the reasons, methods and philosophy behind the life and growth of this church.

Beginning with growth charts #I and II, we notice first, a rapid
membership and attendance growth up to the years 1965 and 1966 respectively. Besides the strong emphasis on prayer; young, energetic and experienced pastoral leadership; and "lay mobilization", all of which will

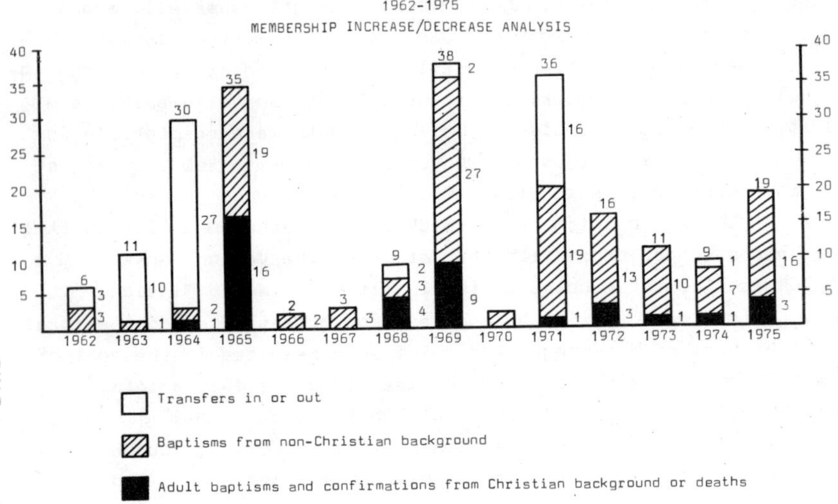

Chart II

Chart III

be treated separately later, there are or may be the following reasons
for this fast growth: a) The early zeal that comes normally with the
founding of a new work, b) a large number of transfers from churches
in south Taiwan and even the west coast in the first three years (see
Chart II), c) fruit of early witnessing (eg. regular street meetings),
and the young people of Christian families being gathered in during
Hudson's four weeks of special meetings in 1965, d) students from the

nearby Mustard Seed school attending services.

Secondly, we observe a decline in attendance growth strangely accompanied by continual good growth in membership. This phenomenon was explained to me in several ways: a) Tank claims "In ten years more than ninety families moved from the Mei-kang Church to other parts of Taiwan."[9] (See third observation, Chart IV) About half of these kept their name on the church roll, but of course did not attend. b) The Mustard Seed school moved and its students, some of whom had become members, no longer attended. c) Some members of outpost churchlets were baptized at Mei-kang and considered members, but did not swell the attendance at the mother church. d) Television cut especially into youth and Sunday evening attendance. e) Inactive members increased with the age of the church and its rise into the middle class. (See occupational and educational categories in Chart VI.)

Thirdly, we notice no "transfers out" or "deaths" recorded on the Membership Increase/Decrease Chart (II). Poor record keeping in this department did not make such possible, but a careful breakdown by the pastor of the 1975 official handbook membership list of 209 persons revealed the following picture:

Study away from home	15	In the army	2
Work in another city, but family still here	14	Overseas	3
Moved or non-resident in Hwalien		"Sunday morning" Christians	25
- moved address known	46	Resident inactive	15
- in churchlets	13	Quite active members	69
- unknown destination	6	Deceased	1

Chart IV

This means that only 109 are resident members, 34 "may" be only temporarily away, and 65 have moved or are permanently residing in other areas. Upon analyzing the 65 a little more carefully, it was found that 17 had already transferred their membership, which leaves an actual 1975 membership of 192. The total accumulative number of adults baptized and youth confirmed over the years is 232. Six (estimated) of these passed away. This means 117, or over half of the members have moved over the years or are non-resident.

This is not a bad record in a city which is known as a "stopover" between the rural areas on the east coast and the big cities[10] of the North, West and South. Often some of the best and most progressive members leave.[11]

A fourth observation needs to be made regarding the "proportion" of transfer, non-Christian background and Christian background growth (Chart II). The last six years have seen little transfer growth, which forestalls the accusation of "sheep-stealing" made by some. The large proportion of baptisms from non-Christian background in recent years reflects its aggressive evangelism. The pastor's wife has the names right now of over forty seekers from non-Christian backgrounds who are already involved in various activities in the church[12] and who could be baptized, but are in many cases waiting for the passing away of an older-generation loved one who is opposed to the baptism. This writer raised a question about the small number (9) of confirmations in the last five years. Were they losing their young people? At first there was no satisfactory answer. An age analysis (Chart V) of the church showed a reasonably healthy situation. Then the pastor's wife discovered over twenty active high school youth who were basically qualified to be confirmed, but had not been gathered in for two reasons: a) The pastor and his wife have not been so involved with the youth recently because of their Saturday evening (Mei-kang's youth night) obligation at Kwo-fu-li. b) Some of these young people fear they may not measure up to certain church membership requirements[13] such as attending a minimum of two church meetings a week, passing a stiff oral confirmation exam,[14] etc. This writer did not have time to investigate the problem further, but attention is already being paid to it as a result of this study and the pastor's wife feels a good number of these will be confirmed with the next baptismal-confirmation group.

Finally, a word needs to be said about the pastoral and missionary leadership in this church. Ladies first. Mrs. Chiang and Mrs. Tank are women with strong, warm personalities, leadership ability, extra-ordinary vision, imaginative creativity and other intriguing characteristics suitable for their kind of work. Mrs. Chiang had four years of training in pharmacy at the Tokyo Girls' College of Pharmacy and two years of Bible and theology evening courses at Japan's Tokyo Theological University. But she feels her new birth and real equipping for the ministry took place in 1938 when she was filled with the Holy Spirit at the age of 18 under the ministry of Dr. John Sung, the world-renowned Chinese evange-

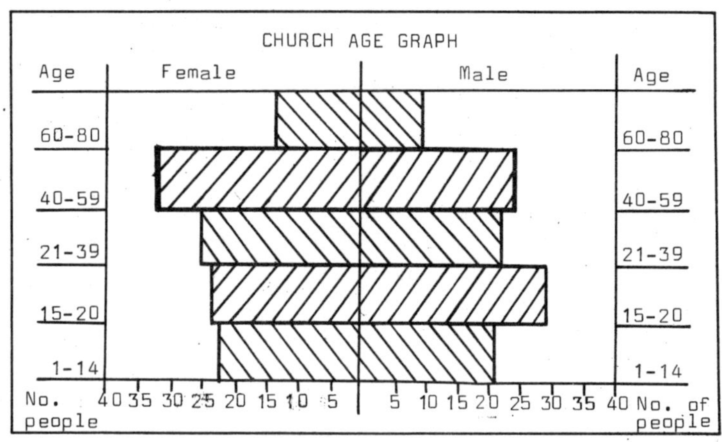

Chart V

list and educator. Mrs. Tank, daughter of Mustard Seed's well-known
Lillian Dickson, was graduated from Wheaton College, attended Columbia
Bible College, and took one year of various courses at Fuller Seminary.
Both women are especially gifted in women's, prison, and evangelistic
work, and active in the full range of the church's ministry. The men's
personalities complement those of their wives very well, they being rather
level-headed, steady, patient and deliberate in manner. Pastor Chiang had
six years of pastoral and one year of teaching experience before he came
to Mei-kang, but again the "difference" in his ministry, his wife claims,
was made by a three-month retreat at Grace College in Pei-ping under Dr.
John Sung's tutelage and a nine months' course at Nan-king Theological
Training Seminary under Dr. Yu Ming Jya's ministry in the year 1947.
Pastor Chiang is very precise and scholarly in his work and has done most
of the basic background research for the graphs and charts in this chapter. Brother Tank, as he is affectionately called, is a graduate of
Ripon College (B.A.) and Fuller Theological Seminary (B.D.), with one
year of study at the latter's School of Church Growth. Besides supervising nine Mustard Seed institutions in the Hwalien area, he is exten-
sively involved in the varied ministries of the church, especially its
outreach. Without the inspirational leadership of these four in a beautiful team appoach, the outreach of Mei-kang Church would be impossible.

PRAYER POWER

The Mei-kang Church was born in prayer and grew through prayer.
During the first five years of the church's life, six o'clock morning
prayer sessions were held daily. Daily prayer with the help of various
"prayer aids" is continually encouraged and practiced. Three or four
times a year all-day prayer chains are held at the church with people
signing up for certain time periods.

Visions, healings, conversions, dramatic answers are attributed to
prayer power. No serious accidents or moral lapses and only five or six
deaths (of old age) occurred in the church over a period of sixteen years
due to prayer, the pastor's wife feels. The quality of Christian life,
the enthusiasm and participation, the many young people attending Bible
schools or seminaries (eg., ten in 1974), and an overall church program
that involves as many as 30 meetings a week[15] are only and basically made
possible through prayer.

How is prayer channelled? Various "Prayer helps" are used. One is
the master list in a book at the church with nearly 200 specific prayer
requests recorded at any one time. Requests answered are publicly and
prayerfully acknowledged in praise and thanksgiving, marked off, and
then replaced by new requests. Another effective aid, widely used in
personal prayer, is a blue note book officially printed by Campus Crusade
in Taiwan. After an inspirational and practical explanation of its prayer method, it has mostly blank pages with one side designated for the
dates and statements of requests and the other the date and manner of the
answer to the request or the reason why the request was not, or has not
yet been answered. The pastor's wife, using this method, recorded 983 spe
cific answers to prayer over a period of seven months. A third and even
more widely used prayer aid is a little hand-sized booklet compiled by
Mrs. Chiang, listing 193 detailed kinds of prayer concerns under such
categories as "nation," "my own family," "our youth group," "conversion
of friends," etc. Over 30,000 copies of this booklet have been printed
and distributed. The booklet is used in personal and public prayer as
a prayer stimulator and guide, and it is especially useful with new converts. But the final, clinching "prayer help" is the definite expectation of sharing the prayer concerns and answers at various fellowship or
prayer meetings or in personal witnessing.

Testimonies to answered prayer are innumerable: goiter dissolved;
eyesight restored; weather changed; articles found; an abusive boss

changed after the Lord put him in the hospital and allowed the abused
Christian to administer the healing medicine;[16] a wife converted during
a typhoon while the Christian husband knelt in prayer out in the storm;
a daughter's receiving a much needed tape recorder, as a result of her
father's winning it as a prize in a golf tournament shortly after the
prayer request was made; the church's needing cleaning and prayer, bringing two workers the same afternoon, all in response to "prayer."

One of Mei-kang's elders felt Mrs. Chiang's prayers were like a net
of blessing and protection covering the whole church, or like threads going out to each member and seeker, gently preventing him or her from
falling into sin and leading him to salvation or a deeper walk with the
Lord. "She is like a computer; her specific prayers help her to understand the needs of each person." Asked whether she was the only one
using this method, the leaders[17] of the church estimated that over twenty
in the church were using the blue booklet and recording their answers.
Many more are involved in other ways of praying.

This writer was immediately put on the prayer list after he started
seriously working on this chapter and felt the warm prayer support. He
also discovered that Mei-kang members work hard to help their prayers
come true. Indeed prayer seems to be the moving force in this church.

LAY MOBILIZATION AND LEADERSHIP

In most churches the load of work is carried by a small number of
people, but even though Mei-kang has thirty meetings a week in ten different places, the pastor's wife says, "We are less busy than most pastors; I only preach four times a week." How is this possible? The answer lies in the training and mobilization of lay leaders and workers.

A careful study of the leadership roles and gifts of 1) 141 Mei-
kang members (Chart VI), 2) about 40 Mei-kang seekers (VI, D), and 3)
local "churchlet" leaders (VI, F) revealed the following distribution
of the five classes[18] of leaders in terms of "gift units:"[19]

   1) Lay leaders serving within the church: elders, deacons, ushers,
      choir members, teachers   118

   2) Lay leaders who reach out into the community to non-Christians
      through visitation, service, and personal evangelism   82

   3) Unpaid or partially paid lay leaders of small groups such as
      Bible studies, house churches, etc.   42

   4) Trained, paid full-time leaders   2

   5) Inter'l, inter-denominational & denominational leaders   5

MEI-KANG CHURCH STATISTICS

A. <u>EDUCATION</u>		D. <u>INQUIRER-SEEKER STATUS</u>		F. <u>LOCAL CHURCHLET LEADERS</u>	
1. None	18	1. Length of time in church:		1. Can preach	9
2. Primary	43	a) Less than 1 yr.	14	2. Can lead a Bible study	4
3. Jr. High	17	b) 1-2 years	19	3. Can teach S.S.	9
4. Sr. High	35	c) 3 yr. or more	5	4. Can visit members	15
5. Vocational	21	2. Church involvement:		5. Lead singing or choir	7
6. University	12	a) visits, does personal work	7		

A. EDUCATION
1. None — 18
2. Primary — 43
3. Jr. High — 17
4. Sr. High — 35
5. Vocational — 21
6. University — 12

B. OCCUPATION
1. Student — 26
2. Housekeeper — 49
3. Factory worker — 21
4. Business person — 16
5. Public servant — 18
6. Hired worker — 9

C. CHURCH POSITION
1. Elder, deacon — 14
2. S.S. teacher — 11
3. Youth officer — 32
4. Miss. society officer — 19
5. Visitation team member — 21
6. Personal worker — 40
7. Church founding worker — 29
8. Choir member — 30

D. INQUIRER-SEEKER STATUS
1. Length of time in church:
   a) Less than 1 yr. — 14
   b) 1-2 years — 19
   c) 3 yr. or more — 5
2. Church involvement:
   a) visits, does personal work — 7
   b) gives testimony — 5
   c) choir member — 21
3. Readiness for membership:
   a) this year — 8
   b) in 6 months — 14
   c) in 1 year — 12
   d) in 2 years — 7

E. FAMILIES WITH CHRISTIANS
1. Only one Christian — 12
2. More than one — 23
3. Whole family — 38

F. LOCAL CHURCHLET LEADERS
1. Can preach — 9
2. Can lead a Bible study — 4
3. Can teach S.S. — 9
4. Can visit members — 15
5. Lead singing or choir — 7

G. 1975 GIVING
1. Sun. A.M. off. $28,592.50
2. Thank offerings $36,684.50
3. Special off. $14,049.50
4. Monthly tithe $150,561.00
5. Church founding fund $37,040.00

TOTAL: $266,927.50

Chart VI

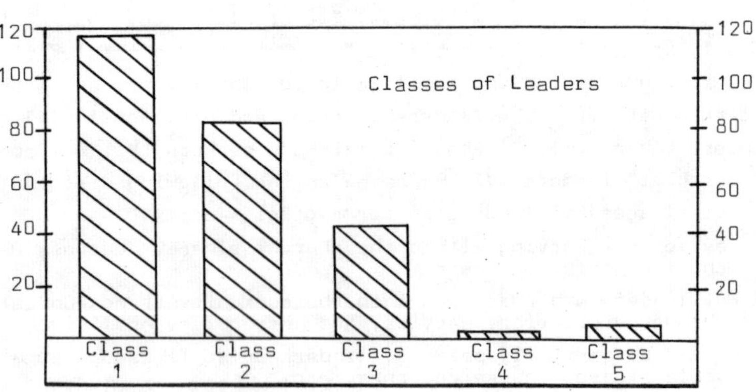

Chart VII

It is rather strange that when many churches on the east coast are
having difficulty finding enough Sunday School teachers, youth workers,
singers and choir leaders, Mei-kang seems to have an over-abundance of
such workers (Class 1). Even more significant are the Class 2 lay leaders. Chart VI, C indicates 21 are able to visit (both non-Christians and
Christians) and 40 are able to do personal work. But when the pastor
carefully checked 141 present members of the church, he estimated that 95
had led at least one person to Christ. Twenty had led "many" to Christ.
Five had led "uncountably many" to Christ; two of these are lay people.
While this is a subjective judgment of the pastor, it says something.
More unusual still is the large number of Class 3 lay leaders. This
writer analyzed the last official six months Church Work Schedule (Nov.,
1976 - Mar., 1977). Of the 46 various speakers, or house church and Bible study leaders, 12 were pastors, missionaries, or able leaders from
other churches, but 34 were their own workers. Subtracting the Tanks and
Chiangs, we have a total of 30 lay workers who are Class 3 lay leaders.
Add to this the 13 local "churchlet" leaders who are able to lead small
groups and the total rises to 43. In Class 5 we have three laymen who
have held or are holding positions on their denominational committees,
and the Chiangs and Rev. Tank who have been or are involved in such work.

The big question is "how" so many lay people have been mobilized.
Here are some of the secrets this writer has detected: 1) The Chiangs
and Tanks somehow have projected the image that the Lord's work is the
most beautiful, happy, normal, adventurous and important thing a person
can do. 2) Everyone is expected to work and is put to work. As one
elder put it, "Division of labour and cooperation is the main strength
of this church. It would be unthinkable not to work. We all dare to do
it." 3) The conviction seems to be that lay people can do more than
usher, take offerings, teach Sunday School and sit on church boards, as
important as these are. Evangelism is their main mission and can be
accomplished by them. 4) The pastoral-missionary leaders have the gift
of delegating work, even to outsiders. "The pastor's wife is very good
at 'catching' (enlisting) people and arranging work," said one man. 5)
New Christians are encouraged to share their prayer answers and their
conversion testimonies right from the beginning, not only at church meetings, but also at the jail, in personal work, and in the outpost churchlets. Not only does this shame some of the older "tired" members into
action, but it helps new converts personally to grow, and supplies the

church with a constant stream of new workers. 6) Small "informal" Bible
study group meetings involve laymen in two ways. A whole chapter of the
Bible is read verse-by-verse, each person taking his turn. After this
the group leader, instead of giving a long formal discourse, encourages
group members to discuss, to question, to share and to testify. 7) The
"team approach" in Christian work is used, giving the new participant
security on the one hand and practical observation of "how it's done" on
the other. This writer went with a group of five to make a hospital call.
The patient was out, but the group began to witness in a pleasant way to
a couple in the same room. The wife replied they were "...worshipping the
gods." "We all used to do that, but not any more. We found Someone
Greater," was the group response. Tracts and a brief testimony were left
with them. A good object lesson. 8) A strong "visitation" program is
practiced. For example, every Friday morning, every church family and eve
seeker family is visited by lay visitation teams. Visitation is also
stressed in the outpost churchlets, but is not carried out as much as
earlier. 9) The simple challenge of a large amount of "concrete work"
that has to be done encourages participation. Members used to be given
a sign-up sheet with 35 different kinds of jobs listed and be asked to
check those for which they wished to volunteer. 10) More "structured
training" programs for various tasks are either set up or attended. James
Tai of Campus Crusade was invited twice for four to seven days to train
people in personal evangelism and this is not a theoretical training
course. Over 200 attended each time, including those from other churches.
The pastor attended "Explo 74" in Korea for further evangelism training
and experience. Sunday School teachers' and youth leaders' training
camps or workshops are attended. Paul Boschman presented Japan's experiments in church growth,[20] and people were asked to write down, for purposes of witnessing, the names of their non-Christian relatives, friends,
neighbours, and fellow workers with whom they are in natural contact.
Thus Mei-kang's people are kept abreast of helpful developments in evangelism.

CHURCH FOUNDING PHILOSOPHY

Between 1955 and 1960 when pastor Chiang was the supervising "cir-
cuit riding" minister to over 100 mountain churches on the east coast,
he and his wife had the vision of starting a Taiwanese church at "every"
railroad station along the coast. The failure of their tangerine orchard,

the income from which was to go for initial support for these churches,
laid this dream temporarily to rest. In the meantime they founded the
Mei-kang Church.

But by 1969 several factors combined to re-awaken the church-found-
ing dream. Their own church had reached a certain maturity, but was not
growing as dramatically as in the early days. During this time also a
good number of the little rural churches were closing down for lack of
funds and workers. The Presbyterian Church drastically cut back its
support for the east coast plains churches, and many people were moving
to the big cities. Nevertheless the Chiangs felt the trend should be in
the opposite direction. Not only should churches be prevented from dis-
solving, but new ones should be founded since there were still many
plains' people along the east coast who had not been evangelized.

At this time a philosophy of church planting and cultivating began
to take shape. With their own church attendance leveling off, Mrs. Chiang
remembered other churches that had had 40, 80 or 120 members for years
without growing or reaching out. Could it be that the potential of those
who would believe in those areas and in her own immediate church community
had been exhausted? Did not Jesus' Parable of The Soils teach that perhaps only one quarter of the people in a given area would respond favor-
ably to the Gospel? So the idea came to her, that if you sowed the Gospel in more areas you would reap more "quarters." Therefore the more
churches you plant, the more fruit you harvest.

When she shared her vision with others, she was told that "It takes
land, a building, chairs, pulpit, etc., to found just one church. How
will you start many?" "Then we'll start in homes, and prayerfully leave
the rest to the Lord," was her answer. And so the idea of house churches
became part of their church founding philosophy. The Tanks came back
from Fuller with similar ideas and the "two-churchlets-a-year" goal was
set. God not only opened homes, but He caused local people to donate
land and buildings for churches. Financially, Mei-kang Church and the
Tanks provided partial salaries and/or travel expenses for certain workers. Even today Mei-kang prefers to invest in people rather than buildings.[21]

Most Mei-kang Church members are happy with the church extension
work, but a few feel that some things are neglected at home because so
much energy is directed outward. Others have voiced the concern that
the "churchlets" have become too dependent on Mei-kang workers and are

not becoming independent and reproducing themselves soon enough. Still others feel that more visiting by both Mei-kang and local workers should be done. To this writer it seems the balance is about right at this time, since Mei-kang workers go only one day a week to each place and the local believers still have to take care of Sunday School work and often Sunday morning services. The idea is to stimulate and not to dominate, to coax and train and not to take over or to be always doing things for them. Perhaps a little more emphasis on training of local resident leaders would be helpful.

CONCLUDING EVALUATION

In conclusion it might be helpful to summarize the factors that have made for church growth, as well as those areas that need further attention. Church growth strengths include the following:

1) Belief in the efficacy and practice of prayer for church growth.

2) The conviction that all God's children have gifts and need to be involved.

3) The ability and willingness to delegate work and to work hard.

4) Big "vision" and the setting of "specific goals" to be reached.

5) Openness to using modern aids, charts, training programs, and techniques to reach these goals (strategy).

6) Willingness to "measure" progress, to evaluate work, and to be critical of self. Pastor Chiang, one of the earliest pastors on the east coast to use a growth chart, when told it might make the church look bad, retorted, "We still need to know where we are."

7) Flexibility to change programs if needed (Mei-kang to "churchlets" to jail - (organic growth)).

8) Emphasis on people rather than buildings.

9) Good teamwork between missionaries and national workers.

10) A humble, unpretentious approach which has helped the church to reach more of the non-Christian "masses."

Areas of church life needing attention include:

1) The small number of comfirmations over the years (Chart II). If confirmations are not considered important or young people are allowed to take communion without confirmation, this should be clarified. Seekers (Chart VI, D) long involved at church also need study.

2) The 40 non-active and semi-active resident members could be checked out more carefully.

3) The 46 permanently non-resident members' (Chart IV) status should be clarified, and better records kept of those who transfer.

156

4) At testimony and other meetings, care should be taken that the
   Spirit is not dampened on the one hand, nor that meetings be
   dragged out too long on the other.

5) Perhaps a careful evaluation of the church founding and adopting
   ministry is due in terms of a. the effect it has on Mei-kang
   Church, b. the churchlets' own maturing, and c. reaching out to
   new areas or kinds of work.

6) Giving (Chart VI, G). There are 74 wage earners in the congregation, and if an average of $4,000 N.T. income per month per
   person is estimated, with each giving ten percent of his salary,
   the yearly income of the church should be $355,200.00 compared
   with the present $266,927.50. Nevertheless, considering the
   number of inactive members and the church's economic status, and
   comparing its giving with that of other churches of equal size
   on the east coast, its giving is excellent.

In fact, with some sharpening up in the above areas, the church's
future ministry will be even more effective in its work for the salvation
of men and for the glory of God.

FOOTNOTES

[1] The Mei-kang or Meilun Harbour Church should not be confused with the
"Hwalien Harbour Church", which is now sometimes called "Jung-shan
Church."

[2] Most Chinese churches have weekly family meetings which are held at a
different home each week, and consist of singing, Bible study, discussion, prayer and sometimes a light snack.

[3] The "plains' people," in contrast to the "mountain people," are mainly
Taiwanese, who are Chinese people that originally came from the Province
of Fukien on the mainland.

[4] Tank, Vernon W., _Local Church Outreach and Church Growth_. An article
describing the Mei-kang Church extension work, written March, 1974,
and available from Ernest Boehr, Box 60, Miaoli, 360, Taiwan, R.O.C.

[5] A ping is a six by six feet area, i.e. 36 square feet.

[6] Tank, Op. Cit., page 2.

[7] Tank, Ibid.

[8] Taken from the official 1975 Mei-kang Church Handbook, p.10.

[9] Tank, Op. Cit., p.9

[10] In analyzing 52 members who moved, it was found that 22 had moved to
Taipei; 6 to Kaohsiung; 3 to Taichung; 10 to towns near Hwalien; 3 to
the west coast; 1 to Keelung; 1 to Pingtung; and 6 to unknown destina-
tions.

[11] Of 52 who moved, only 6 were lost track of by the pastor, 5 were listed

as attending church occasionally, and the others were very active in
churches in the new areas to which they had moved, many holding leadership positions. One wonders whether those moving to the big cities
could be used as missionaries to start new churches there, since many
are strong Christians.

[12] See Chart VI, D, 2.

[13] Other requirements include: 1) If seekers are still worshipping idols
or ancestors, they must postpone baptism. 2) Idols must be destroyed.
3) Seekers must neither smoke nor drink. 4) The main doctrines of the
Christian faith should be studied.

[14] The candidate is interviewed by a committee of elders, deacons, and
pastor as to his faith, Bible knowledge and Christian experience.

[15] Tank, Op. Cit., p.9.

[16] In Taiwan, even when you are in a hospital, a friend will often re-
commend a medicine or herb in addition to what the doctor prescribes.

[17] This writer had a special meeting with about a dozen of the church's
leaders and older persons.

[18] McGavran, Donald A., and Arn, Win, How to Grow a Church, Glendale,
California, Regal Books Division, GL Publications, 1974, pp. 88-93.

[19] Many leaders have several gifts and are included under several Classes.
Some held certain offices or had certain roles in the past showing
they have the "gifts" or leadership abilities. Hence, "gift units."

[20] Braun, Neil; Boschman, Paul W.; and Yamada, Takashi, Experiments in
Church Growth: Japan, Kobayashi City, Miyazaki, Japan Church Growth
Research Association, 1968.

[21] See Chart VI, G. It should be mentioned here that the "Gospel Car"
which was provided and chauffered by the Tanks was basically also an
investment in man-power, because it took people to these outpost
churches for years. Without it this work would have been quite difficult.

ABOUT THE AUTHOR

Otto Dirks is a missionary serving under the General Conference
Mennonite Mission in Taiwan since 1968, working in the area of church
founding and building, first assisting several smaller churches in the
Taichung area for 5 years and more recently helping in the Hwalien area
where he has pastored the Po-ai Church, helped found the new Fu-an Church
and a Developmental Centre for mentally retarded children. He has a B.A.
degree from the University of Western Ontario, a B.D. degree from Mennoni
Biblical Seminary, Elkhart, Indiana and has completed a year's course wor
for a Masters in Missiology at the School of Church Growth at Fuller Seminary.

Chapter 10

A

CASE STUDY

OF

TRANSFER CHURCH GROWTH

Pastor Chuang & Family

My survey is of the Tung-shang church because of 1) my personal involvement in the ministry there; 2) my intent to encourage my seminary to do more of a church-planting ministry in the future, and 3) my wanting to confirm the possibility of transferring church growth.

The seminary in which I am working is now "planting" another new church and this author is working with an evangelistic team in the same type of church-planting ministry. I go back to the Tung-shang church once a month to have fellowship with the brothers and sisters there. I am satisfied with their growth in many aspects.

I want to thank Mr. David Lee, a seminary student who has provided data on the seminary team while they were working there, and also the pastor of Tung-shang, Mr. Chuang Tien-kao, for providing the statistics and most of the materials. Brother Chuang is presently studying at Chung-tai Seminary in courses in the area of missiology. He is student, friend, brother, and colleague of this author. I, too, wish to thank my good wife, Lucy, who has provided many valuable viewpoints for this article and particularly for her personal involvement in the Tung-shang Sunday School development. Finally, this article is dedicated to everyone involved in the Tung-shang church growth.

BACKGROUND OF THE CHURCH

The Nazarene Tung-shang church is located in Taichung City.
Church-Planting - Two Units Merging Into One.
In October 1972, one of two churches was started by a lay person, Mr. Chang Teh-chuan, burdened with the idea of church-planting. Mr.

Chang's ministry started first as a small worship service in his own
home, then expanded to a youth and adult ministry. The members rented
a house and met once a week; they named the church "The Nazarene Taichung Consecration Hall." Brother Chang was in charge for several
months, then later, he resigned from his original job and delegated
himself to full-time ministry. The congregation moved to several lo-
cations, and eventually, brother Chang felt called to the China Evangelical Seminary to be trained as a full-time worker. For a short time
the church was without a pastor until Pastor Chang moved it to the present address.

In October 1973, the Chung-tai Seminary Student Evangelistic Team,
along with the Child Evangelism, started their campaign in a certain
alley of Tung-shang Road. Later they came across an elderly Christian
couple who, after much prayer, decided to open their home for the meetings until May of 1974, when the group rented a house. They used the
title "Christian Tung-shang Church." It is cared for by the same evangelistic team in addition to two teachers. The seminary provides in all
possible ways, both to support and to enlarge the ministry. By August
of 1975, there were eight people baptized in the name of the Lord, sixteen young people converted, and 35 children came regularly to Sunday
School.

Because these two small churches each had the same vision they began to pool their resources. How could they save the greatest number
for the Lord and yet make the most of every opportunity? After much
prayer, much communing, together with the guidance of the Holy Spirit,
they decided to merge.

On May 2, 1976, at the present address, the first meeting of the
"Nazarene Tung-shang" church was held. They now have a full-time pastor
as well as part-time seminary students who assist in the service. This
"merged" church is growing quantitatively, qualitatively, and organical-
ly. Both pastor and congregation are excited about this new adventure.
Participation in activities, joy in fellowship, praise for provision -
all continue to promote the growth of the church.

Geographic Environment.

The surroundings of the Tung-shang church constitute a new community
which is in the process of urbanization in Taichung City. A new market
has been built; the road has been widened; plans are underway to build a
playground and a primary school. The value of the land has increased;

the population figure has soared; department stores have mushroomed.

This was a gospel-barren area - including the nearby community - no pioneering "gospel work" had been done. Some Christians had moved in from the outside area. Soon, however, a few left to join their own denomination. Others quit attending.

From this kind of observation, with this type of knowledge, the Chung-tai Seminary and the Nazarene church began their separate ministries.

ANALYSIS OF THE ETHNIC GROUP

Most of the inhabitants are middle-aged couples. They have their solid foundation in business and enough good savings to buy a new house valued at NT$200,000 to settle down. Their children mostly are in the grade schools and junior high. The oldest would be only up to senior high. These statistics apply to the Mainlanders and the Taiwanese proportionately the same. So, Mandarin-speaking and Taiwanese-speaking are proportionately the same, also.

1. Occupation -

As far as occupation is concerned, the military and government officials and teachers are 35%; businessmen, 25%; industrial workers, 32%; agriculture workers, 3%; and miscellaneous, 5%.

2. Education -

Concerning education, the following statistics resulted: college and over, 5%; senior high, 20%; junior high, 40%; primary grades, 25%; and illiterate, 10%.

3. Family Structure -

The families in the area are classified in the following ways: the large family (over 10 people), 5%; middle family (5-10 people), 35%; small family (2-4 people), 45%; non-structured family (fluid population in which outsiders come to work and business), 15%.

4. Religious Background -

Religion is classified as follows: Buddhism, 29%; Taoism, 21%; Ancestoral worship, 36%; Catholicism, 1%; Protestant, 2%; non-religious, 10%. (Statistics are provided by the Pei-Twun district county, 1976)

THE GROWTH OF THE CHURCH

1. Statistics of the Growth - Adult Ministry (see diagram 1)

From October 1972 to June 1973, there have been eight communicants, 31 seekers (those who have heard the gospel, but not yet baptized), total 39. By June 1974 there were 16 communicants, 38 seekers, total 54. By June 1975 there were 22 communicants, 38 seekers, total 60. In June 1976 there were 41 communicants and 40 seekers totalling 81. The offerings increased. In 1975 the monthly average of income was NT$3,000. In 1976, NT$6,000, double after one year.

2. Statistics of the Growth - Youth Ministry (see diagram 2)

In 1973 the average weekly attendance was 18 people. In 1974 the average was 25. By 1975 it was 28 and in 1976 the membership was 50, but the average attendance was 32.

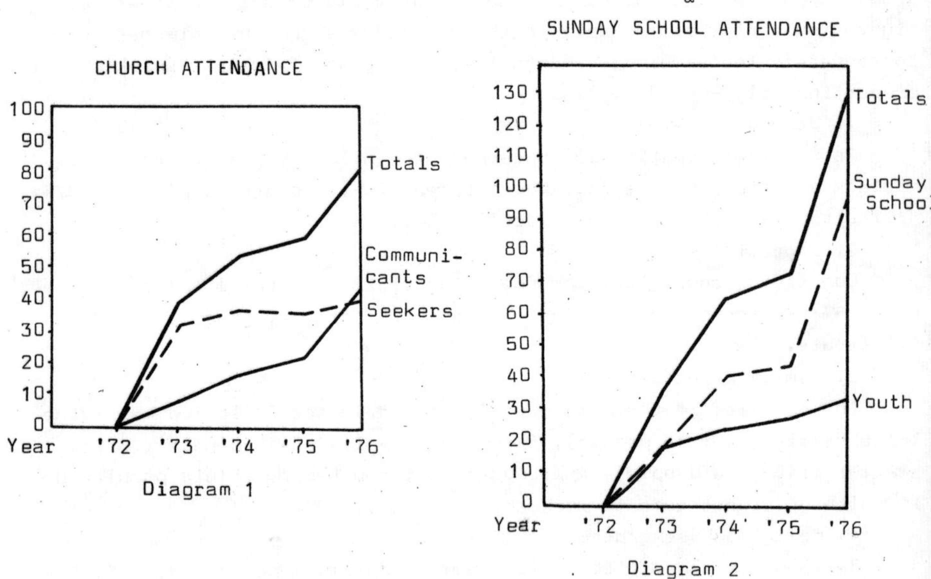

3. Statistics of the Growth - Children's Sunday School (see diag. 2)

In 1973 the average attendance was 18 and in 1974 it was 41. In 1975 44 and in 1976 it was 100 children. Since October 1976 the church has held the branch Sunday School and the open air child evangelism. (see

diagram 3)

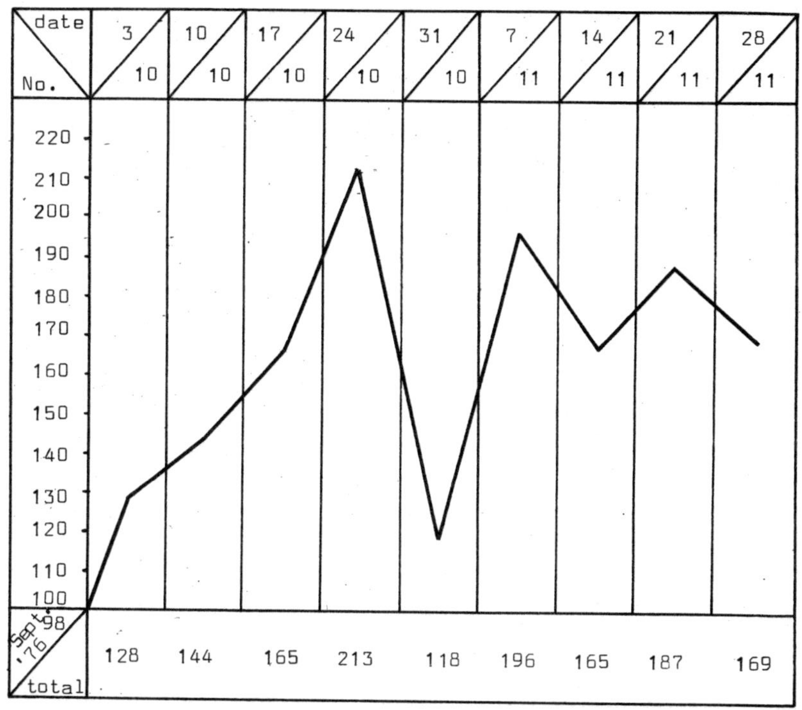

Diagram 3

ANALYSIS OF THE GROWTH

The selection of the right locality, the good spirit of teamwork,
diligent service, plus the seminary 'teachers' joining the project and
the cooperation of the believers as well as the power of the Holy Spirit
are, we feel, the elements which have caused the church to grow.

As the result of a community survey, we located the children of
Sunday School and also the young people in order to learn of their fam-

ily background. We also found several backsliders and were able to
bring them back into the fellowship.

1. Youth Ministry -

The youth ministry grows because of careful planning. For example,
the annual goal, quarterly emphasis, monthly theme and the contents of
the weekly service, the arrangement of speakers and invitation of the
newcomers and also the fruits of the three big crusades (April 17, 1975,
April 24, 1976, November 20, 1976) have contributed to the growth of the
youth ministry.

2. Children's Sunday School Ministry -

The children's Sunday School grows, we believe, because of organization and good planning, because of the teachers' training, the quality
materials used, and the cooperation of the staff members. Due to the
limitation of the location, we decided to set up a branch center in the
kindergarten playground, beginning October, 1976. On Saturday afternoons, the average attendance is 63. In that same community we also
started another open-air child evangelism meeting every Sunday afternoon. The average attendance is now 42.

3. Teachers' Training -

As for teachers' training, in addition to the seminary students'
working in the capacity as Sunday School teachers, the church itself
continues to train her own youth to join the staff. Presently there
are 11 young people who attended a teachers' training workshop, but
only six of them have taken the responsibility of teaching. The other
five are assistants.

PERSONALITIES INVOLVED IN GROWTH

The following personalities are an illustration of some of the
people involved in the growth of the Tung-shang church.

The Pastor

The present pastor is Chuang Tien-kao. (Page 159) He was born
in Kingmoi; was graduated from the Nazarene Theological College in Taipei and is presently studying Missiology at Chung-tai Theological College. He used to pastor a Nazarene church in Taipei before he was
transferred to this church. He is trying with almost ceaseless effort
to promote the growth of the church. Mrs. Chuang was also born in
Kingmoi and worked with the pastor as his assistant. They have two sons

both in grade school.

The Deacon

Mr. and Mrs. Tsao Ing-tsai (Picture B) were born in Hopei. He used
to work in the censorship bureau at Shalu. After retirement, they moved
to the neighborhood of the Tung-Shang market. They met the seminary students who were doing their community survey. They were happy to open
up their own home for meetings. This is the model-method for New Testament evangelism (Rom. 16:5, I Cor. 16:19, Col. 4:15, Philm. 2). The
Tsao's play a very important role in the growth of the whole church.

New Converts

This is an illustration of family conversion. Brother Hsu Wan-rung
and his family (Picture C) were non-believers before they met the students from the seminary. Mrs. Hsu was first converted and then led her
husband and children to the Lord. The whole family was baptized on
August 24, 1975. Brother Hsu, born in Kingsu, now serves in the army
hospital and also attends a theological extension class at Chung-tai
Theological College. He is also the treasurer of the church. Mrs. Hsu
is one of the church deaconesses. Their daughter, Sophia, is teaching
the Sunday School. The whole family earnestly serves the Lord.

B. Mr. & Mrs. Tsao Ing-tsai

C. Brother Hsu Wan-rung & Family

THE PERSPECTIVE OF THE CHURCH

The church plans to be self-sufficient (including having their own building, not renting one) by 1980. The plan is as follows:

1. Increasing the numbers. The church has its own goal to increase up to 100 communicants by 1980. The steps for this are as follows: a) Set up home churches - the church will recruit believers and their families in the vicinity to be willing to open their houses for home meetings. The hosts will take responsibility and the pastor will train them to preside over the meeting, to lead the singing, to go on visitation, to do some preaching and to hold Bible study. He also will evaluate the methods. This kind of a meeting could be held any time during the week, so that all might come back to worship together on Sundays. b) Advocate family evangelism - each family unit pray for one another, show concern in visitation, and the pastor will train them to do personal evangelism using a study guide.

2. Increasing the offering. By 1980 this church should reach self-sufficiency. They have received a subsidy from the Nazarene headquarters, about half their monthly income. They therefore plan to increase their monthly offerings in the following ways: a) Encourage congregation to have monthly contributions - there are 27 adults joining this program. b) Special offerings like Thanksgiving, Christmas, Easter offerings, anointment flask offering (Luke 7:37), Theological Education Fund offering, Religious Education Fund offering, Missions offering. The church has already started these special offerings.

THE YOUTH MINISTRY

The church hopes to multiply the numbers of the youth. Let young people lead their peers. This is a strategy of a homogeneous unit. The reinforcement of the counseling ministry is to train young people to participate in church activities. The theme for the winter of 1976 was "To be the Soldier of Christ." Contents were: 1) the equipment of the Christian soldier; 2) tactics of the Christian soldier; 3) discipline of Christian soldiers, and 4) organization of the Christian soldiers. A young people's crusade is to be held every quarter.

THE SUNDAY SCHOOL PERSPECTIVE

The number attending Sunday School has been tremendous and has over-

flowed the church. The church will, therefore, concentrate on the quality not quantity. On the otherhand, they will continue to train teachers,
to encourage them to attend workshops and to invest in theological education by extension programs, in order that they might have deeper roots in
the Bible and use more effective teaching methods. Special attention is
put on the sixth graders, encouraging them to attend junior high fellowship lest they go astray after graduation from the children's Sunday School.

THE PRINCIPLES & PROCEDURES OF CHURCH GROWTH

After we have studied this case of merging church phenomena, we
can draw some principles to put into a model that can be used by any one
who is interested in church growth.

1. The dynamics of the church growth is the spiritual power of the
Holy Spirit along with a sound biblical belief. In this critical age
we are surrounded by heresies. The church should stand upon a proper
foundation of faith to be sent to the society, to transform, but not to
conform to it.

2. Each church leader/teacher should be aware of his/her own limitation in evangelism and aware of the receptivity of the seeker. He
must survey different kinds of cultural background, sociological phenomena, and population growth; he needs to concentrate on the receptive
areas and so on. This is a principle of priority.

3. When the children's Sunday School overflows the church, thought
must be taken in terms of extension - the open-air evangelism; the setting up of a new branch center. The church should revise the traditional
"come-to" approach to be balanced by a "go-in-witness" thrust. Both are
important.

4. The church should emphasize both reach-out and follow-up. This
includes the qualitative and quantitative growth of the church. The
church should pay attention to possible problems and try to work out
the solutions.

5. The organizations of the church should keep precise statistics -
weekly attendance, offering, decision making, baptism, communicants,
seekers, evangelism, revival meetings, Bible studies, prayer meetings,
etc. This will help future evaluation.

6. The best church growth typology is family evangelism. When a
"chief" of the household is converted he is able to lead the rest of the
family to the Lord to result in a "people movement."

7. Pay attention to the homogeneous unit. There is a stronger sense of affinity when the living customs, moral system and thinking type are in common.. In the pioneering stage of the church the leader should try to avoid the complexity of mixing cultures.

8. Church-planting ministry could start from home meetings and then when it expands to some extent, the church could rent and then build its own building. If the church has been moved to too many places it will affect the spiritual growth of the congregation and also the attendance. For example, often when a church becomes too large for its building it will become self-satisfied - no longer reaching out. Even when the building is packed the next step is to think to give birth to a daughter church (extension growth).

9. A seminary should help in the church-planting ministry along with the coordination of a local church. This is very relevant to the Tung-shang church. This also could give seminary students a foretaste of pioneering evangelism.

10. Small churches in one area, under some special circumstances, should consider to cooperate with one another in terms of evangelism. They should not become competitive.

CONCLUSION

The Nazarene Tung-shang church is a very young church, many things are yet to be done, projects to be launched, and weaknesses to be corrected. However, the above is an illustration of the merging of two churches, which has turned out, we believe, to be better than one alone. This "merged" church has become self-sufficient; it has thrilled the pastor; the congregation have been given a new vision and the seminary students have learned something through this endeavor. This example given shows an opportunity for missionary enterprise, another illustration of how each can do his part to enlarge the kingdom of God to His uttermost glory!

ABOUT THE AUTHOR

William Yang, Tung-chuan is a native of Taiwan. He holds the Doctor of Missiology degree from Fuller Theological Seminary's School of World Missions. He is currently Dean of the practical theology department of the Central Taiwan Theological College in Taichung. Dr. Yang is a past president of the Taiwan Church Growth Society. He recently published a Chinese/English book, "Basic Principles of Missiology."

CONCLUSION

Alan Gates
Hans Vandenberg

It remains now only to review some of the more basic lessons
which emerge from our study of the ten churches. The reader is
aware of the tentative nature which marks such study. For this reason, many of our observations remain somewhat open-ended awaiting
further research before more conclusive statements can be ventured.
However, all who have borne patiently with us through the explora-
tion of these ten uniquely different churches will agree that a
number of lessons do emerge which need to be stated loud and clear.

At the risk of sounding pedantic, we must first say that in every case we have been reminded that it is God who builds His Church
and that He does so through the labors of faithful and obedient servants.

Though each of the ten churches differs substantially from the
other nine, there has been and continues to be notable growth in
most cases. This in itself is an important lesson for every pastor
and church worker to grasp. Namely, that God is pleased to work
through many differing circumstances using people of widely varying
gifts. Moreover, we have found no single pattern or strategy which
might be set forth as the "model church." In a sense, each of the
ten churches are models demonstrating in ten different situations
how the church can grow and enjoy abundant blessing from God.

In almost all the ten churches, factors influencing growth reflected an utilization of resources entirely indigenous to Taiwan.
This again is good news for Taiwan's churches for it reminds us that
in every place God provides from the land and the people adequate
resources to build His Church. While outside help may be enjoyed

from time to time, the Church need not be crippled without it. This
of course is not to be misunderstood in terms of the broader picture
of missions. Where the church has yet to be planted, of course, outside help is still crucial.

By indigenous resources, we refer primarily to the people, finances and other sources of help to be found in the immediate area in
which the church is planted and growing. For example, we have noted
a number of natural "bridges" by which the Holy Spirit carries the
Gospel from person to person. We have observed other "bridges" which
are helpful in bringing newly contacted people from where they are
into the new and "strange" environment of the church building.

Another overriding principle has been that of intense lay involvement in the life and work of the church. Where every member
bears a particular responsibility and senses that his contribution
has a direct bearing upon the well being of the church, then one may
generally predict a growing church especially where involvement is
accompanied with a deep commitment of concerned love to one another
as members of the body of Christ.

The above is often demonstrated best in those churches which have
developed small groups both inside and outside the four walls of the
church. In terms of potential for contacting future believers, those
small groups meeting in homes and other places out in the neighborhood are extremely important. In one church at least, the attendance
in all the small groups meeting for prayer, Bible study or whatever
was almost double that of the church in the building! The value of
this approach as a kind of "halfway house" or bridge between the world
and the sanctuary becomes very apparent.

In most of the churches studied, effective programs for church
growth were found to be the direct results of the vision and burden
of one man--the pastor. It would be difficult to overstate the importance of this one man in each of the growing churches. Not that
he was a one-man show. Indeed, quite the opposite. Being strong
he was yet aware of potential leadership around him and set his hand
to the development of strong men to share the task. However, the
vision, commitment and sense of confidence inspired by God's chosen
leader has been the key factor to successful growth in nearly every
church studied.

We would add only one more point. At least one of the churches is a beautiful and biblical demonstration of harmonious partnership between national and missionary personnel.

Our study would be neither complete nor fair if we failed to share a number of observations which indicate problem areas even in otherwise healthy churches.

The first is an evident lack of concern on the part of some for the task of keeping careful church growth records. It is strange that in matters of finances the church records are complete and in order, but, in matters of church attendance, numbers of baptisms, losses and gains of members, records are too often both incomplete and inaccurate. Moreover, there appears to be little effort made to analyze statistics as a means of diagnosing the health of the church and current trends in growth. A number of materials are now available in Chinese which could be used with great profit in this area.

In these days of increased mobility, the church must be aware of the community in which it stands. It is possible for a church over a period of time to find itself boxed into a linguistic setting different from the language of the church. Under such conditions, flexibility and preparedness for change is necessary for survival.

The church today must keep abreast of the changing times especially in terms of the programs designed for both believer and unbeliever. While there is no way in which we may compete with current television and the theatre, we must maintain the biblical elements of celebration and festive joy which marked the gatherings of God's people of old. Drab, outdated programs for youth and adults will serve only to empty the church and block growth. This phenomenon is well illustrated by the typical small church which averages about 20 in the Sunday morning worship but is packed out during the visit of a local singing group.

Fellowship meals immediately following morning worship are being used as an effective means of developing closer family-type relationships of mutual love and concern. These "love feasts" are proving equally attractive to believer and non-believer alike.

We noted above, the potential for evangelism and growth arising from a proliferation of small groups. However, if a pastor feels that all church activities must take place within the four walls of the church, this potential can easily be lost.

The churches in these studies have little institutional involvement except in the sense that some reach out to local hospitals and
prisons in their ministry. It needs to be noted, however, that many
churches in Taiwan are developing what one might call a "kindergarten
syndrome." Many small churches of 20 to 30 members may be found
operating kindergartens of 100 to 200 children in size. The kindergarten, per se, is a worthwhile project. No one would question this.
The question needs to be asked, however, where does the kindergarten
fit into the church's priorities? For what purpose is it operated?
Does it contribute to the growth of the church? There are, to be
sure, examples of churches which have successfully used the kindergarten as a bridge into parent's homes and parents are finding Christ.
All too often the kindergarten becomes an appendage operated largely
for the income which it brings in. Even this may not be considered
a problem by some. However, when pastor and wife become tied up
time-wise, other important works of visitation and adult evangelism
suffer, not to mention the problem of incentive for offerings due
to substantial income arising from the church's own kindergarten.
This is in no way a plea to close down kindergarten work, but rather
to be sure that the kindergarten is kept in line with and made to
contribute to the overall growth of the church.

It was mentioned above how important a strong leader is in building a growing church. There can, however, be a problem if that leader
allows the work to grow around himself. Should this happen and the
pastor fail to raise up other strong lay leaders to carry the load
together with him, then the results are predictable. When the pastor,
upon whom the church has leaned, is removed for some reason, then
the work falters and the church declines - a sober lesson to all men
called of God to do great tasks.

Prayer and Scripture are vital factors in the life of the church.
Perhaps the most consistently observed factor in these growing
churches has been the commitment to fervent prayer as well as the
experience of answered prayer. It is here at this point of effectual
prayer that gifts, resources and strategy are placed squarely in the
hands of God recognizing that it is only as He enables, as He uses
His people that growth can be realized. Hand in hand with prayer,
of course, is the careful, faithful use of God's Word in all the ministries of preaching, teaching and healing. When God's Word is

recognized and used as the most immediate avenue for knowing,
loving and serving God, the potential for growth is great.

Finally, it is our hope that this book with all its limitations
will inspire and encourage all who labor for God in the church.

We suggest that the case studies be used as a basis for interaction in small groups, as possible resource material in planning
evangelistic and outreach strategies of the church.

As you read and react, we welcome your feedback which may be
directed to our Church Growth Society here in Taiwan.

May our gracious Lord Jesus Christ who said, "I will build my
Church," add His blessing and presence daily to your life and the
life of your church--His body.

I WILL
BUILD MY CHURCH

Study Guide
Supplement

Index Included

TAIWAN CHURCH GROWTH SOCIETY

CHAPTER ONE

PEACE-AND-JOY PRESBYTERIAN CHURCH:
KEELUNG'S CHURCH WITH OPEN DOORS!

1. What basic important Church Growth principle does
   the An-le Presbyterian Church exemplify?

2. Can you follow the suggestions given on page 27 and
   apply them to your annual membership statistics?
   Do you think that by doing so you will obtain a more
   objective picture of the strength of your church?

3. Can you apply some of the ten points listed on page
   28 to your local church situation? Which points are
   the most practical?

4. Which <u>single</u> factor or reason do you choose to be
   most important for the rise and development of the
   An-le Church?

CHAPTER TWO

HAKKA HOME FELLOWSHIPS

1. Describe the unusual method God used in bring the
   Gospel to this Hakka community? Do you know of
   any similar stories?

2. This community was not without Christians prior to
   the conversion of Mr. Yeh. Who were some of these
   other Hakka Christians?

   Why did their conversion to Christianity not have as
   great an impact upon the community as the conversion
   of Mr. Yeh?

   What was Mr. Yeh's status in the community? Did
   his status have anything to do with his ability to
   bring others to the Lord? How?   Is this scriptural?

   What does this say about one way we ought to spread
   the Gospel?

3. Note closely the people who were baptized in Henglung. What relationships do they have to one
   another? What does this tell us about one good
   method for spreading the Gospel among Hakka people?

   Would this principle also be equally effective among
   other groups in Taiwan? How?

4. During the funeral of old mother Yeh, a number of
   indigenous elements were retained - but modified by
   a Christian witness. Discuss the methods they
   introduced into this funeral? Do you feel this was
   a wise method? Are other Christian churches doing
   anything similar? Ought they?

How did this group of Christians overcome the common
accusation that Christians do not pay proper respect
to the dead?

5. Describe the growth and decline of the Tamapo Christian fellowship? What were the reasons for their
   growth and decline? How could this decline have
   been prevented?

6. Discuss the weaknesses of these fellowships listed
   at the end of the chapter. Do you agree with this
   evaluation? How might some of this "stagnation"
   have been avoided. What does this say to your own
   church?

7. Note that the fact of death played a significant
   part in the growth or decline of these Christian
   fellowships. Discuss the cases where death lead
   to growth. How did it lead to decline?

   What does this tell us about the importance of the
   proper handling of the problem of death? What might
   it tell us about working with other people in Taiwan?

CHAPTER THREE

THE CHUKUANG FREE METHODIST CHURCH STORY
A FAITH EXPERIMENT IN CHURCH GROWTH

1. Who were the persons responsible for the building up
   of this church? What ages and backgrounds did they
   represent?

2. What basic indigenous practices can you discover in
   the story of these churches?

3. Discuss the basic methods used in this type of extension church planting?

4. Write up a list of all the basic church growth principles you discover in this chapter.

   What principles can be applied to your church? How
   could you apply them? Discuss carefully.

CHAPTER FOUR

TOK-HENG PUT-INTO-PRACTICE-CHURCH

1. How does this church start new churches? Describe
   their philosophy and methods. How many churches
   have they planted?

2. Why has the Tok-heng church experienced steady growth?
   Find as many reasons as you can. Discuss.

3. Which of the three types of church growth referred to
   on pages 61-62 is the best, strongest type of growth?
   Why?

4. What mature attitudes do you find among the laity
   that make it easier for this church to grow and plant
   new churches?

5. What qualities in the pastor and his wife contribute
   to the growth of this church?

6. How else does this church reflect a fruitful, healthy
   church?

   What can you and your church learn from this study?

CHAPTER FIVE

THE CHILUNG CHURCH
A CHURCH GROWTH STUDY

1. Many of the Chi-lung Church members have been won
   to Christ as individuals. Others have come to
   Christ because of the witness of a near kinsman
   such as a father, mother, sister, brother,etc. As
   a result, a number of entire families have come to
   Christ and are now welled established in the life
   and outreach of the Chi-lung Church. Discuss this
   kind of "family" evangelism as a key to church
   growth and evaluate the possibilities for the same
   in your own church.

2. Lets assume that your church, like the Chi-lung
   Church has become surrounded by a linguistic group
   other than the one in which you are presently working
   eg. Mainlander church surrounded by Taiwanese speaking Chinese. What strategies would you suggest for
   "bridging over" into the surrounding peoples for
   effective evangelism and church growth?

   If this does not apply to your own church, what
   recommendations would you make to the Chilung
   Church?

3. Much evidence can be found to support the proposi-
   tion that the most important single factor in the
   growth of a church is the pastor. What evidence
   can you draw from the Chilung Church study to veri-
   fy this statement. Of course, we would include a
   pastor's wife together with her husband. (Note that

the above principle may work for growth or stagnation depending on the <u>kind</u> of leadership given.)

4. Notice the great emphasis upon small groups in the Chilung Church. Why does this prove to be a factor for growth and what ideas can you glean for your own church?

5. Discuss the place of prayer and Scripture memory in the Chilung Church. Show how prayer can be an effective way of preparing for evangelistic meetings.

6. If you were the pastor of the Chilung Church, how would you deal with the increasing problems relating to family and marriage, especially among young people? How does this relate to your own church?

CHAPTER SIX

FREEDOM ROAD BAPTIST CHURCH
A CHURCH UNAFRAID OF CHALLENGES

1. Under the section "Historical Development" (pages 89-91)a total of seven different factors are given that contributed to the rapid early growth of this church. Can you find them? Which ones apply to your church?

   Which factors do you feel are the most important for strong church growth?

2. "A Church in Action." What are the three special characteristics that mark all growing churches? Do you agree? Why? How are each of these characteristics evident in this church?

3. What is "community evangelism"? Carefully review each phase of this program. Discuss the following questions:

   a. What is the goal of this program?

   b. What five steps did they use to reach these goals?

   Discuss each step carefully. Can these same things be done in <u>your</u> church?

   c. Why did it become necessary to revise this strategy of community evangelism?

4. What does the statement "growing churches are flexible churches" mean (pg. 96)? Explain from

illustrations in this chapter.

5. What new program did the church introduce into their
   community evangelism outreach? Explain the reason
   for this new approach.

6. How many people were enrolled in this Home Bible
   Study program after the first 12 months?

   How did they reach so many? Study carefully.

   Could your church attain such goals? Why or why not?

7. What impact has this community evangelism and home
   Bible study program made on the Freedom Road Church?

   Do you agree with their evaluation of mass evangelism?

   How is mass evangelism now used in this church?
   Explain why they made this change? How do you use
   mass evangelism? Why?

8. Under "A Summary of Church Growth Factors" (pg.100f)
   discuss the following:

   " "Community Evangelism" alone does not explain the
   growth of Freedom Road Baptist Church." What does
   this mean?

   When God wants to build a church, what is most
   important?

9. Discuss in detail the pastoral qualities necessary for
   church growth.

10. What are the seven congregational qualities of this
    church that contribute to church growth? Which
    factors are also found in your congregation? Does
    your church also grow as well?

11. What are the key program factors that contribute to

church growth?   How many are found in your church?

12. What message does the Free Road Baptist Church have
    for _your_ congregation?

    What church growth goals does your church have?
    What can you learn from this church to help your
    church to grow better?

CHAPTER SEVEN

THE SIN-HENG CHURCH OF KAOHSIUNG
MOTHER OF CHURCHES,
ORGANIZED FOR FRUITFUL ACTION

1. How was the Sin-heng church started? Where did they
   meet for the first ten years? Was this a good plan?
   Why?

2. What did you discover about their record for church
   offerings? How do they use their offerings?
   How does this compare with your church?

3. Review and discuss some of the fellowship groups
   found in this church. Why do they have so many
   groups? Do you believe each group has an important function? Why?

4. Under the heading "The Dynamics of Growth" are listed
   nine church growth factors. Review each of these
   factors one by one and discuss the following questions under each factor:

   a. How important is this factor in the growth of
      a church? How did it aid in the growth of the
      Sin-heng church?

   b. How does this factor apply to your church? How
      can this factor be used to help your church
      grow?

5. What church growth lessons can you learn from the
   Sin-heng church? Make a list and discuss how you
   can apply these lessons in your church.

CHAPTER EIGHT

THE T'UNG-HWA CHURCH OF KEELUNG:
A CHURCH THAT SOWED IN TEARS
AND REAPS WITH SHOUTS OF JOY!

1. Why did Pastor Hsu decide to begin a new work in
Keelung?

2. How did Pastor Hsu begin his ministry? What methods
did he follow in planting the Tung Hwa church? How
were his methods different from the history of your
church?

3. On page 133 is a graph showing how the Gospel flowed
along the lines of family and friendship relationships. This is a key to the growth of the T'ung Hwa
church. Study it carefully. What message does this
graph have for your church?

4. On page 136 are ten main keys to the growth of this
church. Study each point carefully and ask your-
selves the following questions:

   a. How important is this key for the growth of the
   T'ung Hwa church?

   b. Is this an important church growth principle?
   Why or why not?

   c. Is this a growth principle our church ought to
   emphasize more? How can we do this?

5. Before beginning a work in this area, two other
churches had also attempted to begin work. They
both failed. Why did the T'ung Hwa church not fail?
Discuss.

CHAPTER NINE

THE BEAUTIFUL HARBOUR CHURCH
A CHURCH-PLANTING & CULTIVATING CHURCH

1. What are the three striking and somewhat unique
   characteristics of the Mei-kang church which probably qualified it for this study?

2. What clues to Mei-kang's energy and outreach do you
   find in the brief sketch of its history?

3. Why did Mei-kang's attendance growth decline after
   1966?

4. How did prayer power help the Mei-kang Church to
   grow? How could it work for you and your church?

5. What are the chief secrets of lay mobilization that
   this church teaches us?

6. How valid is Mei-kang Church's "Church founding"
   philosophy?

CHAPTER TEN

TUNG-SHANG CHURCH
A CASE STUDY OF TRANSFER CHURCH GROWTH

1. How did this church begin? Where did they first
meet and why?

2. What is a "model-method" for New Testament evangelism? (page 165). Look up the listed Bible passages
and discuss their importance.

3. What goals does the Tung-shang church have for
reaching self-sufficiency by 1980? Discuss each
step.

4. Discuss carefully the 10 church growth principles
listed at the end of the chapter. How do these
principles apply to your church?

5. Do you believe it is better for two small churches
to unite into one stronger church for more effective
evangelism?

Do you know of other such examples of church union?

How could you encourage more of this type of united
effort?

6. What personal qualities in the pastor and his wife
   help account for the amazing growth of this church?

7. What is meant by the term "power encounter" on page
   138? Is this a significant concept? Can this concept assist your church to attain more growth?
   How? Discuss.

8. Winning the whole family _or Christ is also an effective way to eliminate the worship of family idols.
   Are you able to create a similar type of family
   evangelism program?

GENERAL INDEX